For "Herself"

Seafood Fishing for Amateur and Professional

R. C. O'Farrell

Fishing News (Books) Ltd
110 Fleet Street, London EC4A 2JL

PRINTED IN GREAT BRITAIN BY
THE WHITEFRIARS PRESS LTD., LONDON AND TONBRIDGE

Contents

		Page
Chapter 1		
I started job hunting		13
Chapter 2		
My five boats and their points, good and bad		19
Chapter 3		
Pleasant but tough—I "look-see" at the Mediterranean		32
Chapter 4		
Crew problem—so I married one		41
Chapter 5		
About the lobster		45
Chapter 6		
Catching		53
Chapter 7		
More about storing		79
Chapter 8		
Hibernian sandwich		84
Chapter 9		
About the crab		92
Chapter 10		
About the crawfish		99
Chapter 11		
Useful tips on line fishing		104
Chapter 12		
Some successful lures and their use		120

Page

Chapter 13
Many ways of catching fish   127

Chapter 14
Inshore netting gives good results   132

Chapter 15
About other shellfish   148

Chapter 16
Choice of craft   165

Chapter 17
Hints on trawling and netting   175

Chapter 18
Winning full profit from your catch   184

List of Illustrations

		Page
Fig. 1	Twm. "Skilled shipwright and boat-builder"	14
Fig. 2	Mooring equipment	23
Fig. 3	Pot counter	24
Fig. 4	Captive knife grinder	24
Fig. 5	Diagram of creels set in fleet of ten	74
Fig. 6	Leakey pot-hauling winch arrangement	75
Fig. 7	Gibson's method of tail-punching to a code	76
Fig. 8	Diagram of large twin compartment storage box	81
Fig. 9	Kilmakilloge Harbour	85
Fig. 10	Eighteen foot canvas covered Irish fishing "curragh"	88
Fig. 11	Lobster and crawfish seaponds at Cleggan	89
Fig. 12	Movements of tagged crabs released from Sheringham	96
Fig. 13	170 mile track of a tagged female crab	96
Fig. 14	The forerunner of hooks	117
Fig. 15	Shelling a mussel	118
Fig. 16	Rag line or feathered serpent	121
Fig. 17	Mackerel line and spinner	123
Fig. 18	The sprule, murderer and dandy	125
Fig. 19	Cart and tractor shanking	135
Fig. 20	The Stream net	137

		Page
Fig. 21	Flue net and posser	138
Fig. 22	Balk net on riding stake	140
Fig. 23	Salmon Haaf net	141
Fig. 24	Diagrammatic representation of a hoop net and its use	154
Fig. 25	Construction of a prawn creel	156
Fig. 26	Stages in constructing a whelk pot	163
Fig. 27	Baiting needle and pot gaff	170
Fig. 28	Trammel net	176
Fig. 29	Basic knots	180
Fig. 30	Showing formation of netting knot	181
Fig. 31	Mending tears in netting	182

List of Plates

I	The Home Port	65
II	Baiting Table and wave flattener	66
III	*Lotus V*	66
IV	Conor O'Brien's *Saoirse*	67
V	Typical Spanish sardine boat	67
VI	Display of pots	68
VII	Cart shanking on Morecambe Sands	68
VIII	Collection of Leakey's pots	69
IX	Male lobster	70
X	Female berried lobster	71

		Page
XI	French type crawfish pot	72
XII	Modern folding lobster and prawn creels	72
XIII	Experimental lobster pot	105
XIV	Inkwell type of lobster pot	105
XV	Spherical pots at Porth Merediog	106
XVI	The American parlour pot	106
XVII	Hydraulic snatch block	107
XVIII	Spanish type keep basket	107
XIX	The lobster and the Beatle	108
XX	Lobster storage tank at Berwick on Tweed	108
XXI	Selecting lobster from storage tank	109
XXII	The "suture" method of tagging crabs	110
XXIII	A bag of mussels being prepared at Portmadoc	110
XXIV	Divers seeking crawfish	111
XXV	Scampi on Leakey prawn creels	112
XXVI	Prawn traps used aboard *Sweet Home*	112

Foreword

WITH automation racing into our economy, it would seem that in the none too distant future we shall have a fair amount of enforced leisure. For those of us who live near a coastline, wherever it is in the world, there are opportunities for both pleasure and profit if we help ourselves to the free bounty of the oceans.

The purpose of this book is to discuss various methods of inshore fishing that are within the reach of the average "do it yourself" lover of the littoral.

Between the wars I was literally kicked out of the Army by a horse, and in due course I swopped the trade of soldier for that of an inshore fisherman. My only difficulty was finding a home port, and someone who would accept me as an apprentice.

I decided the problem would best be solved by a sea-borne search, so purchased a small yawl and with my mother as crew, set off along the Western Coast in search of a permanent anchorage. Good fortune smiled, and I found a near-derelict fishing port on the Lleyn Peninsular (Plate I).

The port and its few inhabitants were ruled over by an Irishman from Waterford of mature years who at the turn of the century, during a shore celebratory brawl, missed his passage to Liverpool, where he was going to search for work. Apparently he was "patched up" and cared for by a cottage-owning widow and eventually "hung up his hat" behind her door. Twm, for that was his name, was a shipwright by trade, but like me, a fisherman by adoption. He was a man of many skills, one of which was the distillation of an excellent Irish Whiskey, solely for home consumption. I still have his recipe, which is so good, that I include it in this book.

Twm took me under his fin and I started my two-year apprentice-ship. Lobsters from May to September, then on to the herring shoals until November. For the rest of the year the building of honestly traditional small boats, and general maintenance of gear, including the never-ending job of mending herring nets, torn to shreds by grey seals.

When the years of instruction were complete, and my master decided to go on his pension, he sold his gear to me and with his blessings handed over his fishing pitch—I was on my own and the year was 1928. Although the going was tough and results at times very poor, I still regard myself as the richest man I know.

R. C. O'FARRELL.

I Started Job Hunting

I TURNED to the sea for a living many years ago and exchanged the trade of soldier for inshore fisherman. Retirement from the service was forced on me at an early age due to a riding accident which left me with a kinked spine. After a year in Army hospitals in India, where treatment was limited to spine boards, water beds and hope, I was written off as unserviceable and bowed out with a base metal bowler hat—the golden bowlers came at a much later date.

Thrown on my resources for a cure, I went to see a much frowned on—by the medical profession—American osteopath. I limped into his "office" where he unravelled a few muscular and bony knots, with the result that I walked without pain, and upright, to the railway station. Within a month I was storming at the War Office, asking for re-entry, but was turned down.

"All very difficult, old boy, you have been boarded out and, as far as we are concerned, you do not exist."

So I started job hunting. Some friends of mine who made mining equipment wanted a contact man—with a smattering of languages, to represent them in the East. The job entailed six months' training at the works, followed by two-year spells abroad, all entailing continuous travelling.

Although life was interesting and results good, I decided at the end of two years to swallow the Eastern anchor, and see if I could find a living fishing our coastline, as my inbred love of the sea and boats was calling. I bought a small yawl and with my mother as crew set off along the Welsh coast to explore the possibilities.

Ashore one day on a foraging expedition at a tiny and derelict-looking port, we saw a donkey shay being loaded with the contents of a diminutive cottage with its feet in the sea. The tenant, an old pilot, told us that he had finished with the sea and was retiring with a new wife to the flesh pots of the hinterland. Including rates, he told us, the rent was fifty shillings a year.

The Old Pilot's Cottage

The landlord, when contacted, was so surprised to find a tenant with ideas of renovation and repair, that he threw in a

FIG. 1. Twm. "Skilled shipwright and boat-builder . . . mixed up in a pub brawl . . . married the widow who patched him up . . . skilled in lobster potting."

red tiled floor to cover the one of beaten earth. The yawl was sold at a profit (which gave me ideas of future deals) and we moved in.

My next-door-neighbour, an Irishman, Twm (see Fig. 1), a skilled shipwright and boat builder of some seniority, was making a living by combining his trade with lobstering and trammel netting in the summer, and herring fishing in the early

My Five Boats and their Points, Good and Bad

Sɪɴᴄᴇ I started inshore fishing I have owned five boats. All were built to do a job of work, and to my specification. Four of them did not match up to requirements, three being too small and one unwieldy, due to its size.

The fifth, C.O.62, turned out to be ideal for the work which called for a heavily built craft of about 20 feet overall, engined with plenty of reserve power. I was indeed fortunate in the builders, the Crossfield brothers of Conway, who were at the time on the point of retirement. C.O.62 was one of the last boats they built. The brothers, who originally came from Arnside, the home of the Lancashire nobby, had generations of fishing craft know-how behind them. So naturally I did not insult them with a specification, as I knew I would get an immensely strong boat of larch on oak. Materials grown slowly on the mountain-side, ensuring a close grain and minimum of sap wood, would be selected and felled by them. Planking was to be of 1 inch thick larch, on 2 by 2 grown oak sawn timbers doubled to the turn of the bilge, with short sunk decks fore and aft.

My reason for sinking them 6 inches was that it would stop odds and ends falling overboard; also, that in a properly designed—lines were by Donald Munro—open boat, short fore and aft decks have never kept out green water, so there is no point in having them at gunwale height. A centre bulkhead, incorporating a thwart, gave her great rigidity. What varnished bright work there was, was in teak, as I have a horror of the so-called mahogany grown in West Africa. After a couple of seasons' weathering, it stains and pits through the varnish, so deeply that it is impossible to scrape and re-surface. Teak retains its glory for ever, and comes up smiling after re-surfacing. Though upwards of twice the material cost, costs on constructional labour are the same for both timbers.

Teething Troubles

Lobstering on the west coast calls for a good deal of inshore work amongst rocks and in tidal races, so most of the work is done in confused and broken water. I therefore opted for full-bodied sections to give buoyancy in the erratically short and steep seas. Gunwale height was kept to a minimum and the same applied to the draught, as I was working out of a tidal harbour. Fully loaded she drew 2 feet 3 inches aft, on an overall of 20 feet with a beam of 8 feet. She was engined by a Kelvin Ricardo running on petrol only as I dare not chance one of the petrol/paraffin stops while working close inshore.

I went over to the yard for the trials, which ran like silk, but as there were several further jobs to be done on the hull I arranged for them to deliver to Bangor on completion, then take over myself for the homeward run.

As they did not turn up at the appointed time, I telephoned and found that they were unable to start the engine. The magneto was as dead as mutton and no spare was available. The upshot of the matter was that she completed her ignominious journey by road and was dumped on a nearby beach to await the tide and a tow across to her home port. Having nothing better to do while waiting, I gave the engine a furious yank and to my surprise it burst into full song. The following morning it again refused to start, so I stripped the magneto and found it wet with condensation. My next move was to phone the makers, whose chairman was a personal friend. The result was that a back-room boy received orders to come down and put matters right and to stay with us for seven days in case further trouble developed.

Fortunately for him he was an excellent sailor. We found that the designers had gone the whole hog on waterproofing and had made no allowance for air circulation. My previous Kelvin engines were fitted with German Bosch magnetos which had ½-inch holes drilled in the base to allow air circulation. Immediately we made the Lucas Bosch-like, our troubles were over, but I must say my faith in electrics at sea were for ever shaken.

Careful Servicing Saves money

A couple of years later, for peace of mind, I replaced the Kelvin by a 10 h.p. A.V.2 Petter diesel. So far, the heads have not been off, but I have made a point of re-servicing the injectors frequently, which may have a lot to do with it. At the same time I decided to build a small glassed-in shelter right up in the eyes, into which two could double up in some comfort. This contained throttle controls and a steering wheel, from which a wire was coupled to a yoke on the rudder. It proved a warm and joyful time-saver in getting in and out to the grounds. The engine could be opened flat out and although water was coming aboard and sousing everything, including the engine, the crew were both warm and dry. We certainly could not have chanced this with a magneto-fired engine.

The teak used for the shelter framing came from the fore-deck of H.M.S. *Conway*, that came to such an ignominious end on the rocky banks of the Menai Straits.

Originally, we hauled our pots over a universal fairlead, aptly christened by Twm, "Armstrong's patent", but tiring of this graft, I looked around for some form of power-driven capstan to do the work. While I was drafting out a take-off to transmit the power, a friend of mine came up with the idea of hydraulics. This certainly appealed, as I could dispense with noisy shafting and gears but the idea was impracticable be-cause of the expense. I found that even if I could obtain a suitable hauler, it would cost well over a hundred pounds.

A few days later, however, my friend turned up with a hydraulic pump and motor he had salvaged from a scrap yard, together with several odds and ends including some one-eighth plate which he had cut out and welded into a capstan head carrier. The final result of the mock-up worked surprisingly well and turned for several years without attention.

This had a happy sequel for my hydraulically-minded friend, who had thrown in the engineering rat race of London with the idea that he might take a leaf out of my rather dog-eared book and have a shot at inshore fishing. Quite honestly, I could give him little encouragement as at that time lobster stocks were dropping and we were starting to over-fish. Also it is bad form to muscle in, commercially, on grounds in use. Of course, the lobsterman has no objection to anyone fishing a pot or two for home consumption, providing they keep clear of his immediate vicinity. I pointed out that there was also the question of capital, with him a minus quantity, but I was able to suggest one or two methods of making the barest of livings on the littoral until something better turned up.

He Started a Business

The whole problem was resolved in the shape of my hauler, when enquiries started to roll in as to where it could be obtained. He took over a derelict cowshed and installed some second-hand machinery on credit, and, of necessity, any orders he won had to be accompanied by ready cash. Within a year he had moved to new premises and installed machinery that had to work to very fine limits, turning out a range of marine hydraulic equipment. Every spare penny was ploughed back into the business, and today he uses a Bentley for transport and is fitting out a 50-foot yawl for a world cruise.

Naturally this has not been achieved without a good deal of mental and ulcerous strain. He still thinks I am the richest man he knows and, oddly enough, I agree with him.

One of the most useful pieces of equipment I have on board is a method of mooring which can be operated without going forrard (see Fig. 2). This I can thoroughly recommend for almost any small craft, especially those fitted with fore-decks. It consists of a length of chain made fast to the Samson post, led through the bow fairlead and along to a point on the gunwale aft of the shelter where it is housed in one of the two chain stops or "devil's fingers". It remains in this position when the boat is off moorings. The bridle, which is connected to the ground chain, is made fast to the buoy by a couple of fathoms of lighter chain.

Useful Ideas

When at mooring the buoy is recovered followed by the bridle which is slotted into the other chain stop. This gives a temporary hold while both ends of the chains, which are fitted with rings, are connected together at leisure by a sizeable screw shackle. To prevent this coming undone a small clip hook or sail hank is loosely wired to one of the chain ends and slipped winter. We had much in common. He had fallen in love with the old port as a young man. When taking passage on a coaster that had put in for shelter on its way from Waterford to Liverpool, he got himself mixed up in a pub brawl, missed his passage, and later married the house-owning widow who patched him up. Twm gradually took me under his fin and I progressed from a "stand and hold it" to a full-blown mate with a minority interest in the takings. It took a couple of busy, informative years to attain this status.

Building a Boat

I also absorbed the basic principles of boat building. These ranged over the selection of growing timber, hill-grown larch for planking, straight-grained oak for timbers, and wind-tortured oak crooks for stems and knees. Twm was very conservative about lobster pots. It was quite below his dignity to make them. They were of willow, made in Cornwall, and were of the ink-pot, or top-entrance type. His specification included some wire reinforcement with very wide top spouts. "Easy come, easy go, catch 'em while they're feeding" was his dictum. For this reason we slogged around under oars every possible tide slack God sent.

Twm's oars are worthy of mention. Made by himself of ash with narrow blades, they were weighted by lead run into holes alongside the inboard handgrips, until they nearly balanced in the rowlocks. This balance removed the wasted effort in down-pressing to lift the blade clear of the water. A spare oar, known as "God's oar" was carried, lashed under the thwarts, in case of damage or loss.

Twm's lobster boat, a beamy, flat-floored 15-footer of clinker build, carried a diminutive mizzen that kept her head on when working, and helped quite a bit in progress when the wind was behind the quarter.

He set his pots with great accuracy on sand in near vicinity to lobster-holding rocks. The reason for this is that lobsters do not forage afar for food. They seem to be quite happy to lie up and wait until it comes to them, living on what plankton they can sieve out of the passing current. This assumption was later proved by a skin-diving friend who found two lobsters lying up in the same hole. He took a baited pot down and placed it within their easy reach, and marked the bedfellows by pinching off the port feeler of one and the starboard of the other. Although the pot took other lobsters, we waited five days before one of those marked moved in. The other, although we left the pot alongside, was still lying up two weeks afterwards. She was heavily in spawn so we left her in peace.

Towards the end of September on this storm-bound coast, a series of gales invariably blows up, and it was necessary at the first hint to get all gear ashore for winter keeping. Pot lines— Twm made them himself by spinning hay rick twine—marker floats and pots were washed off in fresh water, repaired and stowed in an airy shed. This job done, Twm turned his mind to other things.

Twm's Three Fevers

He suffered from three fevers—lobsters, herrings and a yearly search for any family that he may have left behind in Ireland. This, we thought, was an excuse for a spectacular intake of alcohol on his native heath. Apart from this annual jag he was most abstemious. When he returned, always on the fourteenth day after his costly spree, he brought back propitiatory presents. On one occasion he turned up with a pair of brass bedstead ends for his wife, a bottle of poteen (illicit Irish whiskey) for my mother, and a sprig off a shillalah bush for me.

The secret of how he financed these outbursts died with him when he met his tragic end. Possibly the truth lies in one of the many enemy-action bodies that were washed up during World War I. One may have been a purser whose last act before going over the side might have been the removal of the contents of the ship's safe.

On his return, it took Twm a whole week to get back to his delightful self. Most of it was spent on the point, gazing seawards for herring signs—a combination of seabird behaviour, water colour, wind direction and the phase of the moon. Immediately the signs added up to shoaling herring, he shed his melancholia, and out came nets, marker buoys and anchors. We were off at last light to set a couple of trial nets.

On completion of the exercise, we returned home to smoke, and sup Twm's delicious brew of tea that was forever sizzling on the hob in a large enamel teapot. Tea was added as necessary and leaves reluctantly emptied about once a week. Twm had ideas on tobacco. Of shag he maintained that, "you want to be after smoking plenty in the house, the way it will not blow away in the wind". At sea or outside, he favoured twist "the way the wind will keep fire in it". How right he was.

We Peddled our Wares

After the nets had had a couple of hours' darkness over them we returned to inspect them. If the catch was light, we under-ran them, stripped any fish and left the nets to fish until first light. If, on the other hand, herring had struck in any quantity, the gear and fish would be dumped into the boat, taken ashore and shaken out after dawn. In times of plenty we would find the corked headlines sunk with the weight of fish and market prices at rock-bottom. At the beginning of the season, when catches were light, we got about six shillings a local "long hundred", our outlets being shops and pedlars, but during gluts our usual outlets fell out of the market, and we were forced to load up and peddle our wares around the inland villages and farms, the occupants of which took, at the right price, quantities for salting down. The term "long hundred", in fact, denoted a count of 120. On our rounds we usually met up with a mate of Twm's, one Will Rowlands, ex-Guardsman, who travelled the country with a pony cart full of crocks and salt. Will spent most of his day in the pubs awaiting custom, and would challenge anyone—loser pays—to sup, at one go, the full of beer of one of his flower-bedecked chamber pots. He found few takers but many fillers and viewers, including ourselves.

The farmers were a tight-fisted lot and, although we were willing to trade at four shillings a long hundred, we invariably had to close the deal by taking part payment in potatoes or other produce. On one occasion, Twm took half a sack of barley, which surprised me as I knew he had no hens. Driving home in our dilapidated van he told me that he wanted the barley "the way he could be after showing me how to make something to keep out the cold". Later on the barley was laid out on the floor of our store, watered and allowed to sprout, then oven dried into malt. This was tipped into a well-scoured tub, together with treacle, unsalted butter and, surprisingly, a

small piece of soap which according to Twm was "to help the
mash to bubble and work". Boiling spring-water was poured
over it, and when cool, a large piece of toast carrying a handful
of yeast was floated on the top. The mash was allowed to work
for about ten days until fermentation had ceased. In the mean-
time he had knocked up a form of still out of a five-gallon oil
drum in which the mash was allowed to simmer, and condense
itself through a coil of copper pipe.

The resultant spirit was of a strength that would resuscitate
the near-dead—on one occasion it actually did.

Amongst my most treasured possessions is the original
recipe written by, or for, one of his forbears in the seventeen
hundreds. It is headed, "Enough for a Wedding".

> 140 lb. of malt
> 170 lb. of sugar
>   1 lb. of butter (no salt)
>   1½ oz. hops
>   ½ oz. pure soap.

It is followed by detailed instructions which I do not propose
to give as they might rob the Chancellor of his very unjust
duties on our enjoyment.

My Five Boats and their Points, Good and Bad

SINCE I started inshore fishing I have owned five boats. All were built to do a job of work, and to my specification. Four of them did not match up to requirements, three being too small and one unwieldy, due to its size.

The fifth, C.O.62, turned out to be ideal for the work which called for a heavily built craft of about 20 feet overall, engined with plenty of reserve power. I was indeed fortunate in the builders, the Crossfield brothers of Conway, who were at the time on the point of retirement. C.O.62 was one of the last boats they built. The brothers, who originally came from Arnside, the home of the Lancashire nobby, had generations of fishing craft know-how behind them. So naturally I did not insult them with a specification, as I knew I would get an immensely strong boat of larch on oak. Materials grown slowly on the mountain-side, ensuring a close grain and minimum of sap wood, would be selected and felled by them. Planking was to be of 1 inch thick larch, on 2 by 2 grown oak sawn timbers doubled to the turn of the bilge, with short sunk decks fore and aft.

My reason for sinking them 6 inches was that it would stop odds and ends falling overboard; also, that in a properly designed—lines were by Donald Munro—open boat, short fore and aft decks have never kept out green water, so there is no point in having them at gunwale height. A centre bulkhead, incorporating a thwart, gave her great rigidity. What varnished bright work there was, was in teak, as I have a horror of the so-called mahogany grown in West Africa. After a couple of seasons' weathering, it stains and pits through the varnish, so deeply that it is impossible to scrape and re-surface. Teak retains its glory for ever, and comes up smiling after re-surfacing. Though upwards of twice the material cost, costs on constructional labour are the same for both timbers.

Teething Troubles

Lobstering on the west coast calls for a good deal of inshore work amongst rocks and in tidal races, so most of the work is done in confused and broken water. I therefore opted for full-bodied sections to give buoyancy in the erratically short and steep seas. Gunwale height was kept to a minimum and the same applied to the draught, as I was working out of a tidal harbour. Fully loaded she drew 2 feet 3 inches aft, on an overall of 20 feet with a beam of 8 feet. She was engined by a Kelvin Ricardo running on petrol only as I dare not chance one of the petrol/paraffin stops while working close inshore.

I went over to the yard for the trials, which ran like silk, but as there were several further jobs to be done on the hull I arranged for them to deliver to Bangor on completion, then take over myself for the homeward run.

As they did not turn up at the appointed time, I telephoned and found that they were unable to start the engine. The magneto was as dead as mutton and no spare was available. The upshot of the matter was that she completed her ignominious journey by road and was dumped on a nearby beach to await the tide and a tow across to her home port. Having nothing better to do while waiting, I gave the engine a furious yank and to my surprise it burst into full song. The following morning it again refused to start, so I stripped the magneto and found it wet with condensation. My next move was to phone the makers, whose chairman was a personal friend. The result was that a back-room boy received orders to come down and put matters right and to stay with us for seven days in case further trouble developed.

Fortunately for him he was an excellent sailor. We found that the designers had gone the whole hog on waterproofing and had made no allowance for air circulation. My previous Kelvin engines were fitted with German Bosch magnetos which had $\frac{1}{2}$-inch holes drilled in the base to allow air circulation. Immediately we made the Lucas Bosch-like, our troubles were over, but I must say my faith in electrics at sea were for ever shaken.

Careful Servicing Saves money

A couple of years later, for peace of mind, I replaced the Kelvin by a 10 h.p. A.V.2 Petter diesel. So far, the heads have not been off, but I have made a point of re-servicing the injectors frequently, which may have a lot to do with it. At the same time I decided to build a small glassed-in shelter right up in the eyes, into which two could double up in some comfort. This contained throttle controls and a steering wheel, from which a wire was coupled to a yoke on the rudder. It proved a warm and joyful time-saver in getting in and out to the grounds. The engine could be opened flat out and although water was coming aboard and sousing everything, including the engine, the crew were both warm and dry. We certainly could not have chanced this with a magneto-fired engine.

The teak used for the shelter framing came from the fore-deck of H.M.S. *Conway*, that came to such an ignominious end on the rocky banks of the Menai Straits.

Originally, we hauled our pots over a universal fairlead, aptly christened by Twm, "Armstrong's patent", but tiring of this graft, I looked around for some form of power-driven capstan to do the work. While I was drafting out a take-off to transmit the power, a friend of mine came up with the idea of hydraulics. This certainly appealed, as I could dispense with noisy shafting and gears but the idea was impracticable because of the expense. I found that even if I could obtain a suitable hauler, it would cost well over a hundred pounds.

A few days later, however, my friend turned up with a hydraulic pump and motor he had salvaged from a scrap yard, together with several odds and ends including some one-eighth plate which he had cut out and welded into a capstan head carrier. The final result of the mock-up worked surprisingly well and turned for several years without attention.

This had a happy sequel for my hydraulically-minded friend, who had thrown in the engineering rat race of London with the idea that he might take a leaf out of my rather dog-eared book and have a shot at inshore fishing. Quite honestly, I could give him little encouragement as at that time lobster stocks were dropping and we were starting to over-fish. Also it is bad form to muscle in, commercially, on grounds in use. Of course, the lobsterman has no objection to anyone fishing a pot or two for home consumption, providing they keep clear of his immediate vicinity. I pointed out that there was also the question of capital, with him a minus quantity, but I was able to suggest one or two methods of making the barest of livings on the littoral until something better turned up.

He Started a Business

The whole problem was resolved in the shape of my hauler, when enquiries started to roll in as to where it could be obtained. He took over a derelict cowshed and installed some second-hand machinery on credit, and, of necessity, any orders he won had to be accompanied by ready cash. Within a year he had moved to new premises and installed machinery that had to work to very fine limits, turning out a range of marine hydraulic equipment. Every spare penny was ploughed back into the business, and today he uses a Bentley for transport and is fitting out a 50-foot yawl for a world cruise.

Naturally this has not been achieved without a good deal of mental and ulcerous strain. He still thinks I am the richest man he knows and, oddly enough, I agree with him.

One of the most useful pieces of equipment I have on board is a method of mooring which can be operated without going forrard (see Fig. 2). This I can thoroughly recommend for almost any small craft, especially those fitted with fore-decks. It consists of a length of chain made fast to the Samson post, led through the bow fairlead and along to a point on the gunwale aft of the shelter where it is housed in one of the two chain stops or "devil's fingers". It remains in this position when the boat is off moorings. The bridle, which is connected to the ground chain, is made fast to the buoy by a couple of fathoms of lighter chain.

Useful Ideas

When at mooring the buoy is recovered followed by the bridle which is slotted into the other chain stop. This gives a temporary hold while both ends of the chains, which are fitted with rings, are connected together at leisure by a sizeable screw shackle. To prevent this coming undone a small clip hook or sail hank is loosely wired to one of the chain ends and slipped through the shackle eye. It may, however, be necessary to enlarge the eye to allow easy access. When the exercise is completed, both chains, now one, are cast off and the buoy

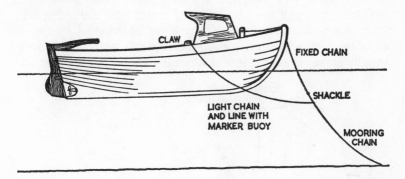

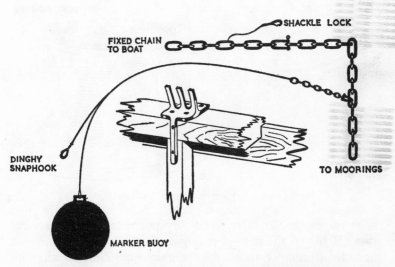

FIG. 2. Mooring equipment. Top: the craft moored; Bottom: detailed close-up. "I can thoroughly recommend this mooring equipment for any small craft".

retained aboard. The reason for a light chain being necessary for recovery is that a buoy rope might well chafe away on the forefoot. A good deal of back bending was countered by the fitting of a strong baiting table at gunwale height. It had a hundred and one uses for jobs about the boat—notably bait cutting.

Two other time-saving ideas were a cribbage type pot counter (see A in Figs. 3 and 4) and a captive knife stone (B). A floating pot gaff was also handy. I was always mislaying my knife stone, the most loseable article on board, so I bolted a carborundum wheel on top of the capstan, and as this was usually running at sea, it was a single-handed job to wipe an

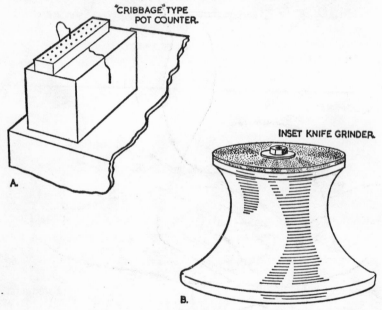

CRIBBAGE" TYPE POT COUNTER.

INSET KNIFE GRINDER.

A.

B.

FIGS. 3 and 4. Captive knife grinder and pot counter.

edge on my knife. After losing my pot recovery gaff several times, I hit on the idea of giving it some buoyancy. This was done by slipping on three corks below the handle. It is still with me.

Protective Fins

In spite of her full bow sections, C.O.62 had a tendency to plunge rather deeply into certain confused sea conditions. At times there were only a couple of inches between her stem and green water. To get over this trouble, I fitted a couple of tapered fins that ran aft for 6 feet about 6 inches above water level. In section they were approximately quarter round and sided about 4 inches at centre. In operation the flat underside acted as a break on the forward plunge while the rounded top allowed for easy recovery on the up stroke. Under normal conditions these fins proved marvellous spray flatteners and made life more pleasant when the craft was under tiller control (see Plate II which is featured in the art section on page 66).

Inshore lobstering lays one open to many rocky touchdowns. This contact invariably occurs at the maximum draught directly below the propeller and in due course may start wearing the protecting skeg, usually a continuation of the keel. Originally C.O.62 had a ⅜-inch keel band continued round the skeg and socketed to take the rudder pintle.

At the end of her second season the band had practically worn through, due greatly to the abrasive action caused when picking up and drying out at moorings. The timber it protected was assuming a crushed look due to a number of rock bounces it had suffered. I took my problem along to the blacksmith, and between us we fabricated a protecting shoe. It was 6 feet overall, tapered to fit the keel over the existing keel band, side bolted through the keel, and as extra support, straps were moulded and fastened through deadwood ahead of the propeller. Materials used were 1-inch iron for the contact part of the box and ½-inch for sides and straps.

Lotus—the Lily

C.O.62 has been the best of faithful friends for many years, and if I were rebuilding there would be few, if any, alterations in design. I might, however, be tempted to paint a pair of Chinese eyes on her bows to let her see her way about. Her name is *Lotus V* (Plate III p. 66). She floats like that lily, but her colours are traditional.

From an early age I was a Captain Slocum fan and the building of my first boat, a 12-foot clinker dinghy, followed very much in the wake of his famous little ship, *Spray*. I, too, found an abandoned and derelict hull hauled out in a field. It was in a parlous state, but when carefully taken apart, nail by nail, the bits and ends served as templates. Fortunately for me, both the keel and stem of oak were in bone-hard condition and served as a backbone to the job. I did, however, make one serious mistake. In my hurry to get on with the job, I entirely forgot to make the necessary shape moulds on which the planking would be wrapped. By guess and by God and with the help of the old transome and thwarts I managed to fair the new planks in. The construction absorbed three school holidays and the result, to the uninitiated, looked like any roughly-built dinghy of her size, though when later I added a lug, she was very much better on one tack than the other. So I must have built a twist or a barmaid's belly into her.

Twm's Survey Methods

This was my last effort in the boat building line until I met my shipwright master, Twm. He had a great reputation along the coast for surveys, and at times allowed me to go along with him for instruction and what help I could give. His method of surveying was to load his pipe and to contemplate the hull from all angles, giving special attention to the sheer-line and what he descriptively termed "barmaid's bellies". While he was doing this the yard, or owner, as the case may be, was removing as much dunnage as possible to allow access to skin and timbers. He would make a start at the keel with a villainous looking little knife and proceed upwards along the planking, feeling for any softness that would indicate rot. If he found any rust bleeding at the fastenings, the stopping would be picked out and nail tested for sickness. Any weeping at caulking would be examined. This done, he went aboard and started with the keel bolts. If it was not possible to draw these for inspection, due to the craft sitting on her keel, he would sound them with a hammer and include in his report that they be drawn and inspected at the first opportunity. The inner skin and timbers were then knifed over in search of any softness. He gave special attention to any places behind lockers, etc., where it was difficult for the air to circulate. If there was any trouble it was usually in these places, especially in forepeak and transom areas. Attention was given to decks and beams at the jointure where rainwater leaks might have caused rot. This completed, he would go top-sides and, if the deck were canvas-covered, short lengths of moulding would be removed and the canvas edging checked for wet rot. He usually found it.

Spars came next on the list, the mast being checked at heel and partners. Vertical shakes did not worry him, but transverse hairlines did, as they were a certain sign of future fracture. Attention was then turned to standing rigging for signs of corrosion which usually occurred directly above the splice. If he thought it necessary, he would cast off—and replace—a seizing. Running gear had its lay untwisted and if the heart was discoloured, written off. Canvas would then be opened out, stitching checked for weakness and material tested for sickness. This was done by piercing at various points with a sharp awl. If on withdrawing the awl the material failed to spring back into shape, it indicated that the useful life of the canvas was drawing to a close. Finally, he would lightly mark with chalk any spots referred to in his survey. I say "lightly" in case the sale might go adrift and the owner could then if he so wished, eradicate signs of a previous survey.

In due course Twm would present a beautifully written report. It had three headings, Seen, Found and Recommended. Sometimes his account for services had an intriguing item. Directly under his standard fee of one guinea—remember it was the hungry 'thirties—would appear "certain considerations" representing a subtraction from the fee if, in his opinion, the time taken did not warrant the full charge, say in the case of a small sailing boat or launch.

It is amazing how many boats are bought without survey and in many cases with dire results. Fortunately for prospective owners insurance companies, having been hard hit in the past, are now calling for surveys, so keep your fist tight closed on your cash until this has been done, otherwise you may find yourself with an un-insurable boat on your hands.

Good Advice Does Pay Off

When shopping around for an underwriter it might be as well to seek the advice of a boatyard or yacht surveyor and ask them to place the business for you. So much the better if they know something about you, your craft and where and how you propose to moor it. This information will be transmitted to the underwriter, and if the agent's opinion is that you are a good bet it will be reflected in the quotation.

One of the oldest companies in smaller craft underwriting is

Navigators and General, who at a guess cover more boats than all other competing companies combined. Their executives are shellbacks to a man, and have a wide appreciation of the troubles that might lie in wait for the amateur. All they ask is that if you get into trouble, act as though you were paying the bill yourself and lose no time in telephoning the details. They even invite you to reverse the charges. In case of a major incident one of their surveyors—they have them in almost every port—will be holding your hand within hours. Their instructions to surveyors are very simple: "See that the yard doing repairs gets a reasonable living and pull out all the stops you can to get our client back on the water."

It is well to remember that marine policies differ from the motor car type in the case of third party claims. The limit of the marine underwriter's liability does not exceed the capital sum for which the craft is covered. To quote a very hypothetical case: you are rowing your dinghy ashore and have the misfortune to inadvertently tap a swimming bread-winner on the head, causing him to sink to the bottom and stay there. It would be quite an easy job for a lawyer to prove negligence—not looking where you were going—and secure judgment for anything up to £30,000, which, as far as I know, is the limit of liability for anything that floats up to a register of 300 tons. This of course includes your dinghy. For quite a small sum you can obtain this extra cover but you must advise your underwriter that you require it.

Good Spirit and Good Faith

Once a claim has to be made the insurers will do all they can to help, provided that the assured co-operates as well. An owner cannot just wash his hands of the whole affair and leave matters entirely to his underwriters. He must do all he can to minimise the loss, acting as though uninsured, and immediately give notice of the casualty. Generally in yacht insurance, because of the essentially personal nature of the business, things go well given goodwill on both sides, and the aim is always to get the vessel back into service again with the least possible delay. Serious disputes are few. This spirit relies on continued good faith between assured and underwriter.

The owner, on his part, must play the game and is under a

duty not only to his insurers but to himself and all on board to make and keep his craft in a sound and seaworthy state, and to use his acquired skill in her navigation and handling. After all, an insurer merely keeps a pool of money fed by premiums and drained by claims. In effect all owners who are insured pay the claims, and therefore the more claims that can be prevented, the more reasonable will the level of premium be kept.

One final word on the safety side. Most small craft claims, in my opinion 70 per cent of them, are the result of faulty moorings. Damages may range from a snorting salvage claim to a total loss. Do not take any moorings on trust unless they are laid by a reputable yard. Watch the most important link of the lot. By this I mean the shackle connecting the up and down or riding bridle to the ground chain. If this is of the screw type it should be riveted over at the thread end and, for luck, a short length of monel or non-ferrous wire rove through the eye and around the shank.

Another safeguard when buying a boat, especially if money is tight, is to spread the cost through hire purchase, or better still, a mortgage. The finance companies, especially those specialising in yacht finance, will make doubly sure that both you and they are the joint owners of a seaworthy and well-constructed craft. In the case of a used boat they will call for a survey and if acceptable may send their surveyor along to see you to discuss any repairs or alterations. It is a well-known fact that craft constructed on traditional lines keep pace with inflation and in most cases prove a very good investment.

Points on Finance

Marine finance is simpler than it sounds. The company only have to satisfy themselves of the soundness of the craft under review and your ability to meet payments. The former is up to them and the latter is covered by a letter from your bank manager.

Commander David F. Johnson, R.N. (Retd), who is in command of the Lombard Banking Yacht Division, has kindly allowed me to make extracts from an article of his that appeared in the *Guardian*. It puts the finance side in a nutshell.

"Basically, marine finance can be arranged in one of two ways, either through the medium of hire purchase, or by a marine mortgage. Although a marine mortgage could be made available for the purchase of a small dinghy, it is not financially advantageous to arrange this form of finance unless the vessel costs at least £1,000. The difference between these two forms of finance is that a marine mortgage can be made available only for yachts that are registered with the Dept. of Trade & Industry, under the British flag. The mortgage takes the form of a loan from the bank to the owner, against the security of the yacht. Security is obtained by registering a marine mortgage against the ship, the registered owner retaining full title. If hire purchase is used, the finance house becomes the owner of the goods being financed.

"Hire purchase is available only for small craft and yachts that are not registered with the Dept. of Trade & Industry. Engines and equipment can also be financed in this manner. It is obligatory for a 33⅓ per cent deposit to be required, the balance being financed over a maximum period of two years.

"With marine mortgage, an owner can expect to borrow up to 75 per cent of the value of his yacht, be she new or used. This money can be raised to purchase the yacht, or for refitting, or other sound, sensible reasons.

The W.F.A. Can Help

If you should think, as I did, of making some sort of living out of inshore fishing, the White Fish Authority's grant and loan scheme as it stands at present might prove of considerable help. As you would be a newcomer to the trade, the Authority would insist that you serve some sort of apprenticeship to ensure that you intend earning a major portion of your future living at the job. At the end of a year or so, if your heart is not broken, you might qualify for assistance towards building and equipping a new boat. The W.F.A. might make an outright grant of 30 per cent of the total *approved* cost of a vessel under 80 foot, and a maximum loan of 50 per cent of the total cost. The purchaser must find the remaining 20 per cent. The rate of interest charged on the loan varies and depends upon the length of the vessel.

I took advantage of this scheme when I re-engined and turned over to diesel and was allowed an outright grant of one-third of engine cost plus installation. In return I had to undertake to make rather copious returns of my fishing. I also undertook to reimburse the Authority if for any reason I sold the boat, or ceased to fish for profit.

Chapter 3

Pleasant but Tough—I "look-see" at the Mediterranean

TOWARDS the end of my second season with Twm he told me that he was seriously thinking of swallowing the anchor and living on his "pension". Therefore, in future I would be on my own, as his fishing would be limited to pottering around for tobacco money.

By this time I had learned enough about the seasonal inshore job to know that it was a pleasant but very tough way of earning a living. My work with Twm was limited to lobster potting, trammel netting for flat fish and some long lining, the less edible products being used for lobster bait. I could see that if I wanted to develop and take some of the tough pully-haulie out of the job, I would have to mechanise and go in search of a mate to share the work, expenses and proceeds. Twm's advice on mates was short and to the point—"marry one".

To widen my horizon on gear and methods that might be usefully employed on my pitch, I decided to spend the winter along the Mediterranean having a look-see and, if possible, working with the inshoremen there. Transport was settled by an offer to crew Conor O'Brien's famous yacht *Saoirse* out of Falmouth towards the Grecian Islands (see Plate IV). She was a brigantine in tabloid form on a water-line of 39 feet. When I joined her she had already circumnavigated the world a couple of times. Illustration of the *Saoirse* appears on page 67.

We Were Sorry for the Steamers

The night before we left I called in for a final drink at a quayside pub and was warned by a pilot that something astronomic in the way of a disturbance was building up on the American side and heading westward. On my return aboard I casually mentioned this to Conor, who had not heard anything about it for the simple reason that *Saoirse* had no wireless receiver. He just didn't believe in them and told me that "if I listened to one of those damned contraptions I'd never leave port". Then he said: "If it's going to blow, let's slip our moorings and catch the ebb down-channel. It will give us sea room." All went well until we were about a hundred miles S.W. of Ushant; then it hit us from the south, gradually backing away towards the north. When things became uncomfortable we hove-to under a backed foresail. Next day the seas became of immense length and height with breaking tops. *Saoirse* corked them beautifully for the next six days, and during that time we blew across several steamer tracks. We were genuinely sorry for the crews of steamers, for we knew of the awful weather that steam would be making of these conditions.

On the seventh night we got into the storm centre, and the sudden shift of wind caused a hell-bent confusion amongst the sea tops, so we decided to strip off the backed forestay sail and let her go under bare poles. While this evolution was being performed, a sea hit us with immense force and neither of us remembered anything until we righted. I was tangled up on the starboard cathead and Conor was towing outboard; fortunately, both of us were on life-lines. When we rid ourselves of the water, we looked aft and saw that flames were coming out of the cabin hatchway. The movement had jerked the primus stove out of its gimbal and broken the burner off. When this had been dealt with, we saw below a complete shambles. Floorboards up, ballast adrift and some rather ominous-looking rusty marks or dents on the underside of the cabin roof. At a guess, *Saoirse* must have nearly stood on her mast-head trucks. We did not arrive at this conclusion—in spite of the primus—until the next morning, when we were checking wind direction on the compass. To our horror we found that the lubber line had capsized aft through 90° so it must have taken a near upside-down toss.

Navy Welcomed us at Gibraltar

Gibraltar was made some two weeks later, during which time we encountered a series of calms and contrary winds. We received a great welcome from the Royal Navy who lost no time in slipping *Saoirse* at the R.N. dockyard. In spite of her immense strength, she was found to be badly shaken and required a major refasten and caulk. This explained the stupendous amount of pumping necessary *en route*. Repairs had to be paid for and as there was a general shortage of ready money, Conor decided to spend the early part of the spring in harbour and earn the money with his pen, and I am indebted to him for the idea. He wrote most acceptable stuff on deep-sea yachting in article form that had a world-wide appeal and sale.

Unfortunately this arrangement did not fit in with the original idea of my seeing as much as I could of Mediterranean inshore methods. Poking round the smaller ports in *Saoirse* would have been an excellent way of doing it, but as this was off I regretfully went over the side and took passage in an old trading ketch, that sailed like a witch, towards Barcelona. There I wanted to have a look at the mussel-farming in the outer harbour and the marketing of deeper sea catches. I paid several visits to the fish market, but was unable to identify most of the fish on sale there. I tried several by the simple method of buying a slice, taking it along to a bar and asking them to cook it. Results on the whole lacked a fishy tang and I found the most tasty and recognisable to be dogfish and tope.

My next move was 60 miles further northward into Catalonia where I had an introduction to a fishing family specialising in sardine fishing and trammelling. I had been offered a cast on a trawler about half-way up the coast to where, with luck, I might be able to catch a local bus to my destination.

They Made Room for My Feet

On arrival there, although the bus was overfull, the passengers, with true Spanish hospitality, pushed up and made room for my feet. There were hard fore and aft seats for about half the complement, so we took it in turns to sit down and, as the floor was full of swaying feet, the sitters had to balance the livestock, consisting of anything from piglets to sacksful of angry chickens, on their knees.

Towards the end of the journey, well beyond the point of no return, we pulled up at a small roadside inn for food and wine, the former consisting of bread, olives and sausage and the wine being passed from hand to hand in large porrons. Just as well that my Barcelona friends had instructed me in the art of porron drinking.

The porron is a glass flask that is filled through the handle and has a pointed spout that, when tipped, directs the wine down one's throat. You start pouring about two inches away from your mouth, then gradually increase the distance to arm's length. The real experts screw their lips into a pea-sized orifice and keep their chin dry.

My fellow passengers fixed me up at a fisherman's bar-cum-eating-cum-lodging house—where a bargain was struck for all services including Continental breakfast and two good meals for the microscopic sum of one and tenpence a day. The fishing fraternity were interested to know that I fished the cold and tempestuous—their words—Atlantic. They bombarded me with questions on methods used· around our coasts, also with invitations to join them at sea and on shore.

For a few days I kept to the latter as all fishing was after nightfall and to join them I had to get on the right side of the police. From what I gathered, they were pretty cagey on the gun-running side, and with foreigners generally. A revolution was to follow.

My request for permission to be sea-borne at night was graciously received and I was instructed to call the following day. This went on for a few days with negligible results, and it was not until they saw me wielding a needle on a torn net that they were convinced I was a fisherman by trade.

I Go Sardine Fishing

My idea was to do a twenty-four hour stint as crewman so it was arranged that I should meet one of the boats when it landed in the morning and work through to the landing the following day. To most of us in this country, sardines are something of a last gastronomic hope out of a tin, or a present for pussy, but this is not so in the Mediterranean countries where, with the ubiquitous olive, it almost competes with bread as the staff of life. It is, however, one of the few Mediterranean fish that responds to straight cooking. Most of the others require an admixture of herbs or sauces to make them table-worthy.

The sardine boats are about 28 feet overall, immensely

heavily built on grown timbers and, with the exception of two hatches that can be tightly closed, are entirely decked in. I was to learn the reason for this later on. They have three closely spaced keels that facilitate both levelling, hauling out—by capstan—and launching. To my surprise there was no pushing during launching. The crew lined both sides and started to rock the boat on her sleepers, timing the rock with an appropriate Catalonian tune. Gradually the forces of gravity took charge and the crew, which consisted of ten men with a further two in the light boat, scrambled aboard. A typical sardine boat is illustrated on page 67.

I arranged to meet one of the boats at 5 a.m. when, with luck, there would be work for a thirteenth man. She arrived at first light with a reasonable catch, and I was put to work on the leg muscle-cracking job of carrying fish boxes through several hundred yards of soft sand to the road, where cannery lorries were waiting.

This job and the ensuing bargaining completed, we adjourned to the local where we broke our fast on laced coffee, crusty bread and a handful of olives. Back again to the boat where the net and other gear had to be unloaded and man-handled to the drying and mending area, again over several hundred yards of the leg-destroying sand.

The net's length was about 400 yards, with a depth of 40 feet. In its wet condition it must have weighed well over half a ton, as it took the complete crew to carry it to the drying area, where the women were waiting with their needles.

This painful operation completed, the boat was hauled up to her beach position. We then broke off for a glass of the district's very drinkable wine, followed by our midday meal and that excellent Spanish custom, the siesta.

The "Light" Method

Early evening found us gathering the net, running the foot or closing rope and placing it carefully aboard for the night's run. The skipper's main concern was the equipment on the light boat, which consisted of a five-gallon pressure tank feeding three large mantled petrol lights that overhung the bow in a davit. When his lights were burning brightly, he gave the order to launch the net boat. The grounds were about a couple of miles offshore, where we came to anchor and streamed off the light boat on its very long painter. A watchman was set to keep in touch with our illuminated skipper, while the rest of us turned in on deck. For bed linen we had a couple of sacks that proved most inadequate for their purpose, in spite of an occasional gulp of a fiery cognac.

I had been told that sardines might strike at any time up till dawn, but that their usual time was after midnight. Negative reports came through until 4 o'clock, when the crew slowly came to life and held a noisy indignation meeting, as most of the other boats had called it a night and were homeward bound and they were all for following suit.

The skipper, however, had other ideas and was expressing them over the water in no uncertain manner. At the height of the recriminations, there was a yell that stilled all others. Sardines had struck the light.

In a flash, a quietness had descended and each man got down to his appointed task with clock-like precision. They cast off the light boat, started the engine, slipped anchor and dropped a weighted dahn buoy, to which one end of the net was attached. The light boat was encircled at an incredible speed with the net running out like a well-behaved roll of ticker tape. Both ends were closed by picking up the dahn and manning foot and head ropes for the final closure. As the circle of corks diminished, the light boat was kept in the centre, ending up alongside in what appeared to be a solid mass of net enclosed sardines. Usually, the catch is baled out with small landing nets but as there were more fish than water, fish baskets manned by two men apiece were pressed into service. Time was not on our side, as a heavy swell out of the south was growing at an alarming rate.

Smothered in Sardines

Our complement of about one hundred boxes was rapidly filled and lashed in tiers along the length of the deck. The remaining space was filled bulwark high. The light boat was filled to capacity but, while recovering the net, thousands of sardines were released.

We then got under way, but a particularly awkward swell increased our list to such an extent that one of the box tiers started to shift. Being nearest, I tried to get my back against it, but it was too late, the others had started to move. I spun round with the idea of stepping into the drink but found my legs pinned to the gunwales. The boat was gradually reaching towards her beam ends, with the water lapping the engine hatch.

To my surprise the list angle had become static, and this gave me a chance to sort out a knife and pass it through the nearest lashings. Away went a couple of eight-box tiers, and to my delight I did not go with them. The list angle then decreased sufficiently to allow me to worm my way up deck to the crew.

By careful re-stowing we got back on a more or less even keel and with thirteen hearts in thirteen mouths we made both beach and history with one of the biggest catches ever.

Due to an onshore wind there was no fishing the following night, so what better excuse for a celebration? I was told the catch, or what remained of it, grossed well over £100, an astronomic figure, so drinks were on the ship. During that twenty-four hours' stint I certainly learned all I wanted to know about sardines. The net result is that I have been unable to look at a sardine, tinned or otherwise, since.

Next I try Trammel Nets

Having been given the freedom of the night, I managed to hitch a lift on a two-man boat of about 15 feet, working trammels. These are really trap nets, consisting of three sheets of netting, the construction of which I will deal with later on. The boat carried four 60-yard trammels weighted to fish on the bottom, plus a couple of single sheet gilling nets for surface setting. A large petrol lamp similar to those used on sardine boats was also carried. As far as I could see its main purpose was working illumination, though my friends assured me that it attracted the small fish, who in their turn attracted the larger ones netwards.

I have an open mind on this point as a few nights later we went out under full moon and the lamp was left ashore with no apparent detriment to the catch. The Mediterranean method of working trammels, due to the tidelessness, is different from ours. There, they are able to stay with them during the hours of darkness and clear them several times during the night. In tidal seas they are usually set across the current and only fish efficiently an hour or so either side of slack water. Our catch, to an Atlantic eye, seemed a rubbishy lot but rather to my surprise, found a ready market.

As time was marching on I decided to set course towards Palma on the island of Majorca where I knew there were a number of small trawlers working out from the quayside. On arrival at Barcelona I found that I was a couple of days ahead of the night boat to Palma, so I spent the time with the mussel-farming fishermen in the outer harbour. For them culture is a laborious business. Spat and immatures are dredged from the bottom, sorted, then hitched to grass ropes suspended from floats or rafts, maturing in anything from six to twelve months. The thin shelled marketables are about $2\frac{1}{2}$ inches overall but lack the flesh and taste of the Atlantic variety.

Working with Trawlers

I spent most of my time at Palma with the trawlermen but managed to snatch a few days with a professional rod fisherman. The trawlers, weatherly little craft of about 40 feet overall, and in my estimation muchly over-manned with a crew of six, worked out at dusk, returning for the dawn market. Their catches beggared description, ranging from a prawn to a tope. In fact, the only fish I could name were members of the dogfish, ray and squid families. The trawls have immensely long cod ends of unbelievably small mesh—just as small as they can be knitted in the size of twine used, so that it is just possible to force one's little finger through the mesh. This sweeping of all and sundry, including immatures, did little damage to the stocks in the days when the boats were under sail and carried their attractive lateen rig, but since changing over to power and increasing trawl size and spread, they are finding catches are down. Even at that time, their seaward searches were increasing, with the result that extra fuel had to be burned on passage. Time, of course, did not matter. Change-over to power would have been all right if they had increased mesh size to let immatures escape. These experiences I describe were in the 'thirties. Even to-day, in the 'sixties, the mesh is still microscopic.

I must admit that during this search for ideas and methods that I could apply at home, I found none that could be of use in our inshore waters. However, my tour started such a liking for the Spanish fisherman and his way of life that whenever possible I spend part of the slack fishing times in his country. After all, living, which I manage to pay for with my pen, is much cheaper there, but as the years pass, the margin decreases. I say I learned nothing. This is not strictly true as I mastered the art of fishing through a bucket, and to gently blow in a fly's face preparatory to swatting it with one finger. The trick of course is to take a sip of brandy between blows!

Chapter 4

Crew Problem—
so I married one

EARLY April found me back at my home port (Plate I p. 65), all set to take delivery of my first fishing boat, which, incidentally, turned out to be mistake No. 1, not in design or performance, but elbow room. In those days small engines were doubtful quantities and as I had to work single-handed the craft had to be rowable. It turned out to be a marvellous little sea boat but far too cramped, especially when I was carrying a small haystack of lobster pots.

At the end of the season she was sold for a handsome profit and with the proceeds I bought a 16-foot launch, quite un-rowable single-handed, but with a lug sail as standby. There was still insufficient room for the gear, and to make matters worse, her side decks made pot-handling a difficult and back-breaking task. She remained with me for one season.

During the next winter I really went to town and ordered, with the aid of my bank, a 30-foot yawl, engined by a 14 h.p. Kelvin Ricardo, designed by Tyrrel Lewis and built by the Crossfield brothers of Conway. She was worked every hour God sent; lobstering, trammelling, mackerelling and trawling. The latter was not a success. We certainly got plenty of fish in the cod end, but spent too much of our time unfastening the trawl from the rock-strewn sea bottom.

By this time I had a most efficient crew, an unpaid one at that, having taken my old master Twm's advice, and married one. She swopped a comfortable easy existence for that of a fishwife, about the toughest way of life I know for a woman.

Among her many duties, she took over (to my joy) the disposal side, and profits took a leap forward. She set her sights pretty high on off-season employment, including property and

41

journalism, but there were two things she flatly refused to do—
mend a net or drive a typewriter.

Even before this I was seldom short of an amateur crew.
One of my slaves was a Naval Commander who hit on the
money-making idea of using *Lotus IV* in her tide-waiting times
as a vehicle for a "nice day for a sail, lady". This he played
entirely off his own bat, turning in the takings to "herself", the
accountant, and mutually liquidating the tips. His rig of the
day was bell bottoms and serge singlet, and his passengers were
regaled with experiences—true and otherwise—ranging from a
back street in Singapore to "who said what to the Lieutenant".
All delivered in the broadest of Yorkshire, his native heath. It
was, of course, Selwyn Rawson, O.B.E.

Lotus IV gave good service for several years, but she was still
not the ideal boat for the job, being difficult to work, due to her
draft, on the main lobster grounds which were close inshore.
War was in the offing and it was necessary to lay up and get
back to the job of soldiering.

Peace was celebrated by the sale of *Lotus IV* at an astronomic
profit, and *Lotus V*, already described, was born.

Then I Met Huw

About this time I had the good fortune to meet Huw, a
man after my own heart. He had retired from the Auxiliary
Coastguard, and we came to a working agreement. Each to
supply his own gear and to share takings after running expenses
were paid. Huw was a most delightful mate. We saw eye
to eye on everything. He had spent his early life on the
Peninsula helping his father who combined lobstering and
smallholding. Later he went to South Wales as a coal-miner,
and collected a minor dose of pneumoconiosis, known as "the
dust". He had the good sense to turn the job in before it was too
late, and looked for employment on the coast. It was now possible to extend our fishing activities further afield and to other
methods. The war years had rested the grounds and had allowed
stocks to build up. Prices were fair, demand good; also cost of
gear replacements had not reached the present high levels that
bear little relation to wholesale prices received for the catch.

We fished very hard indeed when weather conditions
allowed. This wind-gathering side of the coast gets more than

its fair share of windy weather. Rain we welcomed, as it knocked the sea down and, with so much water splashing around, was hardly noticeable. Our clothing, oilskin smocks, topped with an apron and neckcloth, together with high boots, kept us snug and dry. Huw favoured a cap but I settled for an old bowler hat, a tip I picked up from a London river barge-master. It shot the water off and was impervious to flying gear.

I wish I could hand on a few tips about weather forecasting but who am I to lay down laws when our Met. Office with their world-wide scanning frequently make a Charlie of the forecast. In fairness to them, their guesses must cover fairly large areas and although it may be an overall picture, the local weather, due to wedges and what-nots, may not match up to their dire warnings. I have known reasonably quiet fishing weather in my parish when the forecast had predicted distinctly galeworthy weather. It's just a matter of luck, as the whole thing may work in reverse.

Weather Wisdom

Like Conor O'Brien, who refused to have a radio on *Saoirse*, I relied more or less on local signs, mostly cloud formations and old rhymes, but what they portend can vary from district to district. Here are a few of them that I found useful.

> *Red sky at night, shepherd's delight,*
> *Red sky in morning, shepherd's warning.*

Treat the morning red with the greatest respect. Breeze may freshen and glass fall. If red sky at night is accompanied by a dew it usually foretells a day or so of fine weather.

> *If the rain before the wind*
> *Topsails sheets and halliards mind.*

It usually blows up pretty fiercely!

> *Mackerel sky, let your kites fly.*

Denotes wind with no teeth in it.

> *When mist takes to the open sea*
> *Fine weather shipmate it will be.*

All fine and well but take a compass with you unless you want to stay out until the sun eats up the mist.

Two more jingles that I have invariably found true are:

Wind in the East
Blows no good to man nor beast.

Wind in the South
Blows bait into the fishes mouth.

I have never felt particularly friendly towards the barometer, and it seldom enters into my calculations, especially during its minor movements, though I must say that on a few occasions when the bottom suddenly fell out of it, it gave us an hour or two to retrieve our gear. Fortunately my partner Huw was an avid mercury watcher. Twm, who had a word for most things, when asked for a forecast invariably replied "That's God's business. Let's be after taking what he sends"—and we did.

Before we finish with jingles, here are three that will jog your navigational memory.

Meeting head-on

When both lights (red and green) you see ahead
Turn to starboard and show your red.

Crossing

If to starboard red appear
It is your duty to keep clear.

Green to port keeps clear of you.

There are a different set of rules for craft under sail. Generally speaking, power keeps clear of sail.

Chapter 5

About the Lobster

THE true lobster as we know it is, I believe, limited in range on this side of the Atlantic, between the Bay of Biscay and Norway, and on the American side from approximately Maine to Labrador. It is recorded South of Biscay but not in commercial quantities. On the other hand, Crawfish, or spiny lobster, easily recognised by their browny colour and absence of large claws, seem to have the whole world as their oyster and are equally at home in either warm or cool water.

Habitat

For a general picture of the living quarters of lobsters, have a look at an Admiralty Chart, and where the sea bottom is marked "R" (rocks) and "S.T." (stones), it is almost sure to hold lobsters and to some extent crabs, providing the rocks or stones have fissures or undercuts to give cover. Lobsters spend a lot of their lives hiding in holes and presumably subsisting on plankton. This, as you will read later, I have proved—at least to my own satisfaction. Depth of habitat is anyone's guess. The Americans have reported trawl-caught lobsters from a depth of 250 fathoms, and I see no reason to doubt this when one looks at their pressure-resisting armour.

Size again is problematical. There have been press reports of lobsters up to 56 lb. weight—I repeat "press reports". The largest that has come my way was an old warrior of 14lb. but if he had not been short of a crushing claw he would have topped at least 17 lb. Too large to get into a pot, he got himself tangled up in a moored and bottomed herring net in about three fathoms of water. The most interesting point about this lobster was that its shoulder joint where the claw had parted, had calcified or hardened. Normally, lobsters re-grow a claw.

Finding the Grounds

I must stress here that Admiralty Charts will give only a
rough idea of the whereabouts of lobster-holding grounds, as
they were compiled in the dim and distant past, by means of a
greased lead, and naturally, there are many patches of rough
not shown. Most inshore areas, or marks, are known locally, but
it is usually possible to find unfished ground seaward within the
20-fathom line.

When catches eased off on our known marks, my mate
and I rigged an instrument of search, consisting of a 15-ft. by
3-in. galvanised pipe, chain bridled to a towing warp. This was
towed along at about two knots and with a finger on the warp
it was possible to "read" the bottom by feeling the swish of sand,
the rattle of gravel, and bumps that varied in magnitude
indicating stones or rocks.

When the latter were felt, a few baited pots were sent over,
buoyed, and shore bearings were taken. By this method it was
possible to cover far more ground than by the soul-destroying
job of searching with greased lead. It is well to remember that
lobsters do not confine themselves solely to rocky patches. Some
live on rough ground, and by rough I mean a matrix of mud,
gravel and weed, where in some cases a tidal scour has made
suitable hiding places. I am also told, though I have no evidence
of this, that lobsters live on and bury themselves in soft mud, as
do scampi.

The following, I think, proves my contention that lobsters
spend a lot of their time holed up and a minimal amount of time
in search of solids in the way of food. A skin-diving friend of
mine whom I asked to go down to clear some pots, came up with
the information that he had found two lobsters lying side by
side in a hole at the base of a boulder. At my suggestion he took
down a baited pot—a two-eyed east coaster—and set it directly
in front of them, first marking the pair by snipping off ends of
opposing feelers, port on the one and starboard on the other.
The pot was visited two days later and both marked lobsters
were still in position. A stranger, meanwhile, had entered the
pot.

Bad weather prevented diving for the next few days, but when
we resumed, the baited pot was still unoccupied, yet still in full
view of the marked pair.

During the next week the pot was regularly inspected, until one day we found the port lobster had moved in, but as she was in heavy spawn, was returned to the water about 200 yd. away. The final dive took place the following day and much to the diver's surprise, the marked hen was back in her original lodging. Both lobsters were in dark blue hard-shells, so it does appear that in this condition they are able to keep themselves going on the minimum of solids.

The reverse, of course, is the case shortly after shell shedding. They are ravenous and un-marketable and I have known the same lobster return day after day to the same pot. As further proof of this theory, it was arranged to ring a large lobster-holding pinnacle rock with half a dozen pots. They fished well for two or three days, then, although the pots were left down, catches entirely dried up. I asked Mr. Roy Midwinter, one of my skin-diving friends, to go down and report. He surfaced with the information that he had seen three lobsters holed up and two moving on sand at the base of rock. He also reported that as there were so many un-reachable holes, the rock must house a population considerably in excess of what he had seen.

Life in a Tidal Keep

Still not satisfied about the lobster's occasional feeding habits, I constructed a small concrete tidal pond and installed a dozen lobsters, some fractionally over, the others under a pound weight. There was one exception. Although the same size as its companions, it was but half the weight as it had recently shed its shell. To discourage scrapping or cannibalism, claw sinews were surgically dislocated, French fashion. (I will deal with this rather tricky operation later on.) Apparently it takes a week or so to repair the damage, but by that time they have become blood brothers and can live together peacefully.

Each month two lobsters were removed from the tidal pond, carefully weighed, cooked and savoured. Loss of weight during the test was nil to minimal but towards the end of the six-month period there was a hint of flesh drying, but it would have taken a gourmet to spot it. The interesting point about this test is that no food whatsoever was offered and there was only one death, which was due to shell changing. Water temperature during the period ranged from about 40 to 60°F.

Shell Shedding

The lobster that decided to moult during its incarceration, did so at a very convenient time and my wife was indeed fortunate to see the whole operation. Here is her verbatim account:

"I noticed that one of the family was lying on its side and performing the most extraordinary gymnastics. The shell joint between tail and carapace was slowly opening and after a few minutes of struggling the lobster lay perfectly still for about five minutes and I thought it was dead. Then the gymnastics restarted; the tail joint opened wide and the carapace split open longitudinally, allowing the complete inner body to escape, jelly soft and complete to feelers and eyes. The whole operation took some fifteen minutes."

She decided that this luscious feed could not remain with the others, so floated it off on a shovel and placed it in a partitioned section of our indoor aquarium. All went well for a couple of days and the shell started to thinly harden and change colour to the palest of blues. Then disaster struck, and the lobster was found dead one morning. A post-mortem revealed that a tiny crab had squeezed past the partition and eaten its way through the lobster's eye and onwards into its head. The cast shell, perfect in every detail and feather-light, joined our museum.

This was our second failure to protect a moulted lobster. The first was in the case of "George"—a finger-sized specimen to whom we gave the dubious protection of a piece of drainpipe in the aquarium. Unfortunately, another of these murderous little crabs—about half the size of a small fingernail—killed George in exactly the same way.

Reproduction

This is a hard and soft business, aptly described by Prudden in his interesting book *About Lobsters*, published by the Bond Wheelwright Coy. of Freeport, Maine, U.S.A.:

"In the male lobster (Plate IX), the two swimmerets nearest the carapace are hard, sharp and bony, whereas in the female the swimmerets are soft and feathery. The difference is clearly noticeable either by sight or feel. When the female is impregnated by the male, his semen is deposited in a pocket in the underside of his mate's body. The receptacle appears as a shield wedged between the bases of the third pair of walking legs (Plate X), its function is to hold the sperm until the eggs leave the body and are ready for fertilisation. The female is always impregnated by the male while she is soft shelled and often within a few hours of moulting.

"When the female is ready to accept her mate, it is believed that she searches him out. Anderton, in *The Lobsters*, describes the process:

'Two hours after moulting, she was seen roaming round the pond and frequently approaching the various shelters, returning regularly and fearlessly to a shelter containing a large male. On approaching the entrance to this shelter, the large claws were extended in a direct line with the body and the antennae were thrust within the shelter. After a few moments the beak of the male appeared, the female meanwhile rapidly whipping her antennae across the now projected beak of the male, which in turn showed increasing signs of excitement, his antennae being whipped very rapidly over the female in the same manner. After an interval of perhaps a minute, the male gradually withdrew from his shelter, the female at the same time turning over on her back to receive him. The sexual act took place at once, occupying only a few seconds, the male retiring at once to its own shelter and the female into another. The following day both were observed to be living in one shelter and they continued to do so, off and on, for several weeks.'

"The living together does not usually continue except in captivity. The male at mating is almost always hard-shelled. The sperm has great vitality and endures for months and possibly years. Female lobsters of all sizes from eight inches upwards have been found with hard shell and even with newly laid eggs, with their receptacles full of sperm. The sperm remains in the female's body for at least nine months, alive and vigorous until such time as she spawns. To lay her eggs, the female turns on her back and flexes her abdomen into a pocket, the eggs then flow from her genital openings at the bases of the second pair of walking legs in a steady stream into the pocket, passing over the sperm receptacle on the way. At this time the sperm cells leave the receptacle and fertilise the eggs. In this transfer, the eggs are attached to the mother's swimmerets by natural adhesive, to remain throughout the period of incubation. For ten to eleven months the female, now called a "berried lobster", constantly guards her eggs against marauding fish and steadily moves her swimmerets to aerate and clean the eggs. A lobster lays from 3,000 eggs (for a 7-in. female) to 75,000 (for an 18-in. female), 18,000 eggs is about average for 10-in. lobsters (1½ lb.). The eggs resemble Caviar and are about 1/16-in. in diameter. Their colour when freshly laid is black, but as they grow old they become lighter in colour. This is most noticeable towards the close of the period of development.

"The stored yolk of the egg supplies the material for growth; the egg gradually enlarges in size until its membrane bursts, hatching the young lobster. As the mother's instinct is mainly directed to the protection of her eggs, the young disperse as soon as hatched, rising to the surface where they remain for a short time. It is interesting to note that surface-swimming young lobsters often seem to be attracted by light, a trait that is not evident once they become bottom-dwelling."

How Anderton's flirtatious female didn't lose her life as well as her virginity in that tank of presumably hungry lobsters, is indeed a mystery.

Here for the record is a tale told to me by another lobsterman, a keen observer of marine life in the rough. "I spotted a cock lobster, doing as it were, 'sentry go', alongside a known lobster-holding hole, situated on the edge of low springs. The following day he was in the same position, but sitting on and apparently feeding off the remains of a smaller lobster, possibly an amorous intruder. Next day he had disappeared and I assumed that he was in the bridal chamber. Several days later, when the tide allowed, I carefully raked the hole and drew out the female. She was the palest blue in colour with the thinnest of thin shells."

I am left with the thought that nature is marvellous—it is indeed amazing that having satisfied his lust, the cock does not feast on his jellified partner. He would at least have the excuse of getting back unto himself what he had lost and at the same time covering up the lady's shame!

Predators

There is little doubt that the main enemy of mature lobsters is man himself, this being proved by the serious downfall of catches during the last thirty years or so. Demand has risen with our higher standard of living. From this angle, lobsters "have never had it so bad". Considering the immense number of eggs they carry and hatch out, the young must have a fairly rough time in early life from wriggling egg to near-catchable maturity —which is from nine inches overall. Their remains have been found in the stomachs of quite small fish and in the stomach of that arch nuisance, but otherwise delightful animal, the seal (of which I have more to say later on).

Diseases

Like most living things, lobsters suffer from various illnesses. At the time of writing, the Americans seem to be bedevilled by a disease known as Red-tail, and as it may be of interest to keepers of storage ponds, I will quote from a paper of the Sea and Shell Fisheries and Marine Agricultural Experimental Stations.

"During the summer of 1946 an unknown disease became epidemic in many lobster storage ponds along the Maine coast and caused a high mortality amongst the lobsters stored there. At the beginning of the investigation it was believed that this disease could be recognised by a creamy pink or red colouration on the underside of the abdomen, thus the name 'Red-tail'. Later, it was discovered that this red colouration could not be relied on as a symptom, but since the term 'Red-tail' has become so widely known to designate this disease, no attempt was made to change it. Only a microscopic investigation will prove that the disease is present. It shows up in the sharp progressive increase in weak and dead lobsters stored in ponds or tanks, especially after the temperature of the water has reached 45°F. The disease was found to be non-poisonous to human beings and other warm-blooded creatures but highly contagious amongst lobsters. This study further showed that while the lobster is the natural host, the disease organism can live and multiply outside the lobster tissue in the slime of crates, bait barrels and boat tanks; it is also found in the mud of tidal ponds where the infection is known to be present. With the constant discharge of water from infected storage places the organism has been traced for miles until the dilution by the sea itself makes detection impossible. From transmission studies it has been found that healthy lobsters that have devoured weak or dead lobsters and even those that did not have access to diseased tissue but lived in the sea water contaminated by the organism fell victims to the disease."

Feeding Habits

The short answer to the question "What do lobsters eat?" I received during my apprenticeship, and it was very much to the point. "Anything with flesh on it, that has once lived." There is, of course, an exception to every rule. My inherited "potting pitch" extends about six miles either side of my home port. I say inherited, as in our part of Wales, there is a gentle-manly agreement amongst lobstermen to keep clear of each other. In deeper water there is a limited amount of rough ground, which, of course, is "free for all". At the southern end where we join up with our neighbour's pot line, there is, or rather was, due to myxomatosis, a change of food fancy amongst the lobsters. For generations their pots had been baited with skinned rabbit, for the simple reason that it was much easier to catch the infesting rabbit than it was to catch fish.

We tried rabbit on our pitch, mostly a fish-baited one, but found our lobsters turned up their noses at rabbit and as far as they were concerned it could just rot in the pots—which it did.

Chapter 6

Catching

O NE is either snowed under with bait or suffering such a shortage that covetous eyes are flashed on the passing funeral: seldom have I struck a happy medium. Preservation means salt and it has got to be of the right type—the ordinary bar type being practically useless. It must, repeat must, be of a large-grained variety. Fairly finely crushed rock-salt is excellent, and similar salt of the rough-grained variety can be obtained at any of the fishing ports. I cannot advance a reason for this, as all salt must, chemically, be the same. Possibly it has something to do with the slower transformation into brine, thereby making in some way a more thorough job of extracting the water content from fish.

When bait is gathered off-season, it is as well to clean guts and blood away before cutting it up into suitable pieces and layering between rough salt. In this way, it will keep over the winter and, as far as I know, quite a few winters. Bait for use within a few days is cut up and thrown into a couple of boat-borne dustbins containing a wash of brine.

I have also tried with some success roughly smoking the bait, having gutted it and given it a couple of hours in brine. It is strung up in a shed over a smokey fire of oak chips and sawdust and left to sweat overnight. Sometimes the result doubles for both pot and table, and I have found that lobsters share my taste for smoked fish. Its attraction may lie in the down-tide trace of smell, taste or whatever intrigues them—another advantage is that crabs and congers don't like it. But it is as well to know that even this "dainty" will not really attract them potwards until the water is around 50°F. On a descending scale I found the most attractive baits were as follows:

Cormorant. Skinned, gutted and hung in the sun until they are black, then cut up into seven long-lasting and most attractive baits. Possibly, the attraction is due to their fishy and oily tang.

Gurnard. Can be used fresh or thoroughly dry-salted and dried. In the latter case they seem to store indefinitely but are not quite as attractive as fresh. Can be obtained, frozen into blocks and boxed at main fishing ports.

Fresh Bones and Offal. Good, but have to be enclosed in a netted bag.

Salmon Heads, Bass and Mullet. Very attractive due to oiliness of salmon and shiny appearance of bass and mullet.

Herring and Mackerel. Allow to taint a bit, otherwise a suffering of conger and crabs. Rather soft and inclined to wash away if not in a net bag.

Artificial Bait. A good deal of scientific enquiry has gone into the question of long-lasting artificial bait; without, as far as I know, any joy. Why enquire further? Here is the answer. A tin of cat food, with a few holes knocked through the container will slowly release a most attractive oil streak which lasts about seven days and has been found to pay high dividends against capital cost. There may be something in the shininess of the tin, for I found on a recent visit to the Connemara Lobster Fisheries that lobstermen there use concrete, inset, mosaic fashion, with pieces of mirror to weight their pots. I was told the idea came from America.

Another near-artificial bait is a bacon-rib bone, which stores indefinitely and seems to go on catching even when denuded of its minimal meat-scraps and is as bare as the proverbial bone. This point was amply proved to my satisfaction as you will learn later when I discuss the merits of the "parlour pot".

Bait Buying and Catching

It is often possible to buy bait in the form of gurnard or fish offal if working near a fishing port, but this method we found thoroughly unsatisfactory, especially in warm weather, due to the time factors. Merchants gave excellent service, but in spite of crippling transport charges, the railway people usually forgot about it en-route with the result that it stank to high Heaven on arrival.

Our bait came the hard way, by long-lining or netting; long-lining produced mostly Dog, Tope and Skate, with an occasional prime of the flat fish or cod family. Tope and Skate were not found particularly bait-worthy, but there was a reasonable consumers' market locally for skate wings and to some extent Tope, if it was skinned and smuggled into the back door of a Fish and Chip shop.

Long-lines were made up of a hundred or so largish swivel-headed hooks attached to yard-long snoods spaced a couple of fathoms apart on the line and baited with small pieces of mackerel, herring or any other similar fish. These lines are usually set across the tide on a roughish bottom.

If a mixed bag of bait is wanted for the pots, and a certain amount of prime to cash against overheads, that amazingly productive net, the trammel, is the answer. It can be set on the bottom or floated on the surface, in the latter case it is amazing how it attracts salmon or other "shinies".

Excellent results have also been achieved by a shore-set sheet or anchored drift net. Ours were of very fine nylon or Ulstron, giving maximum tangleability, and it is extraordinary how a finger-sized fish will tooth in these materials. The net has an overall length of 60 yd. with a 4-in. (two-in. knot to knot) mesh, fishing 22 meshes deep, normally set into the third, though I prefer it to be nearly the half. By this, I mean 100 yd. stretched and set on ropes to 60 yd., with head line corked and a foot-rope of the new leaded line, "Leaded" means that the lead weighting is incorporated in the line itself which does away with the many snarls caused by individual leads falling through the meshes.

The nets are set about 100 yd. apart at right angles to the beach and attached to stones or anchors. The inshore end of the net should be fairly near the high-tide mark. Ideal conditions are as much flood as possible over the net during the hours of darkness. If the wind is over the land, so much the better, as this discourages weeding. Trammels of course can be set in the same way and pay higher dividends, especially in flat fish if set on the outer ground.

The history of trammel nets is particularly interesting. They were brought over to this country in the days of Elizabeth I, who licensed Frenchmen to fish her rivers. In those days the nets were called "trois mailles"—an apt description of their three-net construction. The trammel or trap net, consists of a curtain of three nets, the two outer and matching ones having a mesh of about 10 inches knot to knot, in either square or diamond formation. The inner net has a mesh of 2-in. knot to knot and is set very baggily, to head- and foot-ropes, both longitudinally and vertically. In fact it is set approximately by half its stretched and vertical depth. Fish striking the inner net trap themselves in the pocket formed by the square or diamond. Though their catching ability is good, unfortunately, their trapping of weed and rubbish is superb. Picking them, especially if the wind is in the East, is one of the beastliest of jobs. Incidentally, I have found that Easterly weather produces poor results in all forms of fishing—even lobsters don't like it. Give me a breeze from the South that is reputed to put the fish on the move and blow the bait into their mouths.

Catching

It is inevitable that borderline immatures will be brought up occasionally, but these can be returned to the water with the minimum of delay if they prove to be undersize. Simply knock two copper nails into the gunwale, with their heads exactly nine inches apart. Measurement of the lobster is then determined by placing the extremities of tail and beak alongside the nails.

There are many ways of catching lobsters, ranging from poking about under a rock to using baited pots or nets. The design and make-up of these pots and nets is multitudinous and ranges from the traditional to the individual's fancy. We lobster-men are full of fancies, but after a lifetime on the job I have settled for the dictum "Easy come, easy go, catch them while they are feeding". This form of fishery entails a good deal of sea time, as it means working all the fairish weather and tides God sends, sometimes with just enough light to see the buoys.

A pot with absurdly large entrances, preferably topsides, must be used in this type of fishery, as this enables the lobsters to fall in easily. Undoubtedly the best is the barrel-shaped wood slatted sort that the French use for Crawfish, with wood-lined (not netted) spouts of about 10 in. diameter (Plate XI). Netted spouts are definitely out, especially if there are crawfish about, as these are inclined to snag on their many body spikes.

As I have already said, there are many ways of catching lobsters, but the queerest I have seen working is a bushy bough of Blackthorn wound round with the product of a couple of woollen stockings. It only requires a stone weight, a piece of bait,

a buoy and you are in business. It is extraordinary how a few
strands of wool will tangle and hold a large lobster or crab.

Another "off-beat" method used by a friend of mine who was
passionately fond of tabled lobsters but not in the least fond of
being sea-borne, involved a number of old drainpipes, which he
set among stones near the bottom of spring tides. In due course
some of these were adopted by lobsters as suitable lairs and
occasionally were cleared out at low tide by means of a hook and
a landing net. We knew him as "Billy Crabs" and he plied his
trade at low springs. His tool consisted of a short broomstick to
which was fastened a bluntly hooked steel rod about 18 in. in
length. Billy knew every hole and cranny within his parish and as
the spring tide fell he would take up position to warn all and
sundry off his pitch, until such time as his holes were accessible.

His method was to feel gently around the hole. If it contained
a lobster, his hook would invariably be attacked, and it was
usually possible to tease or otherwise encourage the lobster
forward where it could be grabbed, from aft, across the carapace.
If it was an immature, he left it severely alone, as these little
brutes can swing their clippers backwards through at least 180
degrees.

Crabs, unlike lobsters do not seem to dislike fresh air and can
be found dried out in crannies well above low water mark.
Lobsters, on the other hand like a little water around them, and
if above low tide mark are usually to be found in rock pools. My
friend Billy had no compunction in feeling around a dried out
fissure for crabs, but was scared stiff about doing the same thing
in a water-filled hole. There might well be a militant lobster
within, or worse still a large conger.

To illustrate this point he told me the mythical tale of a man
who did this and found a conger fastened to his fingers. He was
reputed to have addressed the conger thus: "Let go you silly
bugger, the tides is coming in and we'll both be drowned . . .
and the conger yawned".

Yet another method we used that paid handsome dividends
when our drift of trammel nets were torn beyond reasonable
repair (mostly by seals) was simply to tie a few pieces of bait to
head rope and nets which were then set alongside rough ground
and left down for about a week. Any lobster on the prowl, trying
to get at the bait, tangled himself up in the sheet meshes and

awaited our convenience. As it was impossible to untangle them they had to be cut adrift and the net cobbled up before re-setting. It was unnecessary to re-bait as other fish had conveniently enmeshed themselves. By this method the replacement costs of a new net were usually more than amply met.

The Making of Pots

Unfortunately, the art of traditional potmaking is fast dying out. They are difficult to come by, unless one is lucky enough to know of a constructor and places an order with him well ahead of the lobster season. There are pot makers to be found, but mostly they are in the churchyard.

There is little doubt that in the future lobster and crab pot will, like nets, become products of the factory.

A friend of mine, Mr. Bob Leakey, of Settle, in the middle of Yorkshire, who is by profession a sound abatement engineer, but by inclination a fisherman, foresaw this shortage about ten years ago and decided to set up a village industry. He sent me half a dozen different types to try out and report on. Several were of folding or rather collapsible, construction and others were on strong metal frames. They were either netted with synthetic fibres, such as Courlene, or with plastic-covered diamond mesh wire, and all were fitted with Leakey's patent escape inhibitors. Shapes ranged from the East Coaster in both folding and rigid form (Plate XII) to a sloping sided Cornish type with a bottom that latched out and had the advantage of allowing pots to nest.

I found that the "folders" did not fish as well as the "rigids" and this was due, I think, to a certain looseness (since rectified). They evidently bore out the dictum of my friend Tom Scales of Scarborough, "Pots must lie quiet on the bottom".

Results, in a nutshell, were as follows. The Cornish type fished well ahead of the others, due I think, to its easy-come-hard-to-go escape inhibitor. Well down the course came the inhibited East Coaster, followed by the "folders". The Cornish type were very well constructed and covered with the plastic wire. As far as I know the original test pot is still fishing hereabouts whereas the others have been lost during the past eight years.

Bob Leakey tells me that he has now produced a pot that will catch Dublin Bay prawns (scampi), and from Press reports it seems to be doing very well. First, though, you must find the type of mud that houses these tasty morsels, and when you do, get in touch with Bob who, by the way, has expanded his business into one covering all gear requirements for the inshore-man, from all types of nets to lines. His illustrated price lists are an education in themselves. Not only does he tell you the cost of each item, but also how to use it. It is thoroughly sound advice and makes good reading.

Another rather weird contraption was sent along to me for report. It came from a firm of London importers who were hoping to make a killing with a lobster pot which, in all their innocence, they thought to be nothing short of wonderful. The original maker, whoever he was, must have spent an immense amount of money on press dies. It was of un-reinforced over-supple plastic and looked like a large football split in the middle to form two halves. The two halves were connected with several flimsy latches, the idea being ease of stowability, baiting and removal of lobsters, if any. The mesh in my opinion was too small and gave a good deal of resistance to water and weed. It was just as well that I did not trust the latches, and decided to try them out before setting the pot, for they came adrift when the pot was gently rolled along the shore. Its flimsy construction ruled out fixed ballast, so I settled for pouring about 12-lb. of concrete into the bottom half, with a cast-in-metal ring for attachment. The spout, a plastic cuff, was too small both at outer and inner ends.

After lashing up the latches, the pot was set in reasonably quiet water but it was not seen for a couple of weeks, as it had rolled down-tide and into deeper water from where it was picked up at a low spring. It had caught and held one tiny lobster. On re-setting it suffered an on-shore blow and was never seen again.

I mention this pot for the simple reason that someone may come up with the idea of something to fit into our plastic age, but I would recommend them to try out a few mock-ups of the finished article before going to the expense of dies or moulds. They might also keep in mind the idea of the parlour pot described later.

As already mentioned, methods of constructing pots are legion, so I will confine myself to the more traditional types used both in this country and in other parts of the world.

East Coaster

At one time this two-spouted pot was more or less confined in use to the eastern coasts of England and Scotland, but is now in fairly common use along our western seaboard. The average size is about 27 in. overall by 18 in. wide by 14 in. high. It is made with a slatted bottom, and the bows are preferably of wild rosewood, as this takes most punishment. Failing rosewood, solid cane can be used. Other woods, such as hazel are inclined to rot quickly. The frame is covered with netting, preferably synthetic, and the entrances are on opposing sides. These are set on wire rings of about 5 in. in diameter and are stayed open by attaching to the wooden cross members. In some cases, rings are dispensed with and the inner part of the spout is finished "soft".

In the far north around Orkney, they use a pot of similar design, but favour a single spout. Granted, it may make escape more difficult, but this advantage may be outweighed if the pot rolls over on to the entrance side or if the entrance becomes blocked by weed. The only real advantage I can see is that the Orkney type, being about 8 in. smaller, allows more pots to be carried in the boat. There are a number of variations on this type of pot, mostly relating to spout construction. Some have shrimp net or expanded plastic mesh woven into the spout floors to give easier "walk-in" and there are also weird and wonderful one-way valves to prevent escape. Here again, I have an open mind on these valve affairs, and this goes for most types—apart from "parlours". Valves, whatever their construction, may inhibit escape, though to some extent they must also hinder entry. Many will disagree on this inhibiting business, especially my friend Bob Leakey, of whom more later.

I recall one experimental pot that I tried out (Plate XIII), very nice to look at and handle, but despite its high production costs, it fished no better than our traditional East Coasters.

The East Coaster is a thoroughly good pot, difficult to make, but, providing it has easy spouts and is fished on most tides, there are few to equal it, especially for lobsters. It is also a good crab pot, but in this case the spout should be even wider, as cock crabs grow to an immense size. For Scottish crab fishers the dimensions of the pot are increased to 30 in. long by 16 in. high. A large creel is preferred for crabs as they are caught in greater numbers than lobsters and in times of good fishing the crabs are inclined to pack themselves into pots like undergraduates trying to see how many can get into a telephone kiosk during "Rag Week". When this happens I have noticed a high percentage of immatures (under the legal landing size of 5 in. across the widest part of their carapace) are included.

Talking of crabs reminds me of a character hereabouts who used to make his "baccy" money by collecting these brutes at low tide. His fishing outfit consisted solely of pants, shirt, no boots, and a hooked poker. The interesting part of the operation was that to keep his hands free, he used the bagginess of his shirt, above the belt, as a collecting sack. Before shirting, he anaesthetized them by squirting a spitful of tobacco juice into their faces. In all but the stowing, I have tried this method, and for some reason it works and keeps their limbs folded for an hour or so.

The Cornish Pot

This was the pot favoured by my master during my apprenticeship, but as basketry was beyond his many skills, he ordered them from a Cornish source. They were bulky affairs of 2 ft. or more in diameter, beautifully woven in willow, and costing, as far as I can remember about 6s. apiece, delivered (Plate VI). On grounds of economy, I tried my hand at this basketry business with disastrous results both in shape and sore fingers. Twm was indeed right when he said "leave 'em to the Cornishmen, who have grown up in the trade".

The top entrance, or spout, of the Cornish pot varies from 5 in. to 8 in., depending on whether the quarry is lobster or crab.
The larger entrances are also useful if there are any crawfish about.

In North Wales similar woven pots have been in use, as far as I know, since the early seventeen hundreds, but instead of using willow they employ alder, a much tougher wood (Plate XIV). They are spherical in shape and of immense strength, which enables them to survive a very great deal of inshore buffeting. Being too small to take internal ballast like the Cornish type, three stones or bricks are lashed near the bottom on which they sit comfortably in an upright position.

An interesting point about these pots is the very small size of spout, which is due to the fact that merchants of the past refused other than prime lobsters. In other words, up to $1\frac{1}{2}$ lb. The large ones were un-saleable and the spout was designed to keep them away from the bait. Not a bad idea really, as it left them to get on with the job of reproduction. Nowadays anything of any size will sell, so one can hardly blame the lobsterman for increasing the size of spouts, though in the long run he is quite likely to fish himself out of business, which is exactly what is happening in certain areas. His main hope will be in finding un-fished grounds sea-ward in much deeper water. There is a distinct possibility of this as lobsters have been trawled from considerable depths by the Americans.

The Parlour Pot

It is possible that this type of pot will come increasingly into use on grounds that are being—and it is happening to most—caught up. The pot (Plate XVI) has the advantage of cutting down expensive fishing time, as instead of needing continuous fishing, it can be left down for several days and still hold the catch.

There are several designs, but the one most favoured is a four-bowed East Coaster, with opposing spouts in two of the divisions and an easy cod end leading into the other. The original idea of this pot came from an article in a fishing magazine. I took it over to my pot maker, the late Mr. Tom Scales of Scarborough, who I am glad to say immediately caught on to the idea and based his prototype on the East Coaster plus an extra compartment, which meant another bow.

This pot was left down for a couple of days and as I was suffering from one of those shortages of bait, I used a couple of bacon bones. When raised there were two lobsters in the cod end of the pot, and I was surprised to see that they had taken the bones with them. We tail-punched them for identification and placed them, with the bones, back in the entrance part. When the pot was next raised, the two marked lobsters had been joined by another. All three and bones, which had been picked ivory clean, were returned again to the entrance part. Due to the incidence of bad weather, the pot was not inspected for about a week, after which we found all three lobsters back in the cod end side—together with the bones. One thing that sticks out a mile is that lobsters, if they can escape from a pot, whether to the outside world or to the doubtful safety of the cod end of the pot, invariably take the bait with them.

We used a number of these pots, with marked success, in inaccessible parts of our lobster parish. By "inaccessible", I mean caves or gullies, where it was only possible to pick them up in fair weather. They acted like a child's money box.

Metal Pots

The oldtimer may tell you that lobsters do not like metal pots, maintaining that they "sing" in the water and that lobsters do not like music. This old belief has gone the way of many others. The most successful pot I have ever fished was of metal, but in some way ruled itself out on capital cost. Twenty years ago, made by a professional wire-worker, they cost £4 10s. apiece in dozen lots. Today's price would be anyone's guess. The main advantage was that as long as the buoy rope kept strong the pot was practically unloseable and unbreakable. The framework was $\frac{1}{8}$ in. rod covered by $\frac{1}{8}$ in. wire of $\frac{5}{8}$ in. mesh. There were top and side spouts of oval shape scaling 10 in. by 8 in., and at one end there was a door. The spouts reduced about 2 in. at inner ends, and were fitted with "pigeon traps" one-way wires, counter balanced with a piece of lead to keep them in the down position. They acted as fairly efficient escape inhibitors and it took lobsters about a couple of days to learn the secret. They were also good fish catchers, mostly of the wrasse variety, which were most acceptable bait. In fact, the pots were found to be self-supporting in this way.

I still have one of these pots which has fished on and off for twenty years and I have a winter use for it. It makes an excellent bird table and it ensures that the smaller birds get their rations. With the inhibitors removed they can fly straight through the side spout and use the top ones as an exit. The bigger birds, such as Seagulls and Jackdaws are thus defeated.

Setting

This poses no problem if setting inshore where the shape of rough ground can be seen. The best location is on sand as near to rough as the pot can be placed. I say this, as in my experience even if the pots are dropped a mere 10 yards away fishing will be minimal. Lobsters do not, repeat not, like searching for food far away from their haunts. I cannot understand why, as apart from seals and otters, they don't seem to have, when mature, many underwater enemies. Seals I am absolutely sure about, as on one occasion one was seen to come into shallow water where a wire keep pot was situated. He sculled around the pot for a few minutes and was then seen to be chewing at a lobster. Having dispatched this, he (it was a bull) set about tearing at the pot. He was chased off and on examination the wire pot was found to be severely bent, but its lobster content was complete. The one he had been eating had been discarded the previous day, dead.

Otters may also be a hazard. A lobsterman fishing on the other side of this Peninsula was mystified by the fact that the mesh of some East Coaster pots was always being torn. The mystery was further heightened because the damage occurred only in a limited area. Out for a Sunday walk along the cliff bottom, he stumbled upon the answer when he saw an otter and several of her young sunning themselves. They quickly disappeared into a hole, and upon closer inspection, he discovered quite a number of lobsters shells around the entrance. Being a nature lover, as so many fishermen are, he left the otters in peace and gave the immediate area wide berth with his pots.

Having dealt with setting on the visible bottom, the time will come when the shallows—by shallows I mean up to five fathoms —will be clouded by a stirred-up sea. In these conditions my old master, Twm, who knew the bottom for miles around like the palm of his hand, felt around with a lead line in order that his pots might set comfortably on the edge of the rough. He stuck to inshore grounds, as up to the time I joined him he was single-handed and unable to work a multiple line of pots. The multiple came into the picture later on when by means of the towed pipe, we were able to find rough farther out up to the 20 fathom line. Even when these patches of rough are found and indicated by shore marks, it is imperative, prior to setting the fleet, to feel around with a lead line, otherwise there is every possibility of dumping the pots on open sand. Fair enough, if you are after that more adventurous creature, the crab, but as I have pointed out, this terrain is disliked by the lobster. Fleets containing any number of pots may be set, according to the size of the ground, but for a boat with a two-man crew, a fleet of twelve is considered to be a comfortable size.

PLATE I. The Home Port

(*Photo:* R. Jones (Nefyn) Ltd.)

66

PLATE II. Baiting Table outlined in white as also is the mooring chain and the wave flattener mentioned in the text

PLATE III. Lotus V. Author's favourite craft; painted in traditional colours. For description see text p. 25

PLATE IV. Conor O'Brien's famous yacht Saoirse—a brigantine on which the author sailed to Gibraltar. Conor O'Brien circumnavigated the world twice in this craft.

PLATE V. Typical Spanish sardine boat equipped with lights to lure the fish shoals. On such a craft the author nearly lost his life. (Photo by courtesy of Atlantic Ocean Fisheries)

68

PLATE VI. The traditional round type of Cornish pot is here shown. The other type of pots shown are designed by Leakey. At the top is a standard East Coaster, then a folding creel, and a square based Cornish pot. All are fitted with plastic inhibitors. See text on Catching Lobsters.

PLATE VII. Cart shanking as operated on Morecambe Sands by Billy Burrow. "His horse is kept in finest fettle—for he is the only form of life insurance if one is beaten by the fast-flowing flood." (see text p. 133)

PLATE VIII.   Collection of Leakey's pots showing various types. "Leakey's sales literature is an education in itself", see Chapter 6 on Catching Lobsters.

70

PLATE IX. Male Lobster: a—abdomen; b—beak; cl—big claw; ct—cephalo-thorax (a combination of head plus thorax); ey—eye; fe—long feelers; sf—small feelers; tf—tail fan; wl—walking legs
(From *Practical Hints for Lobster Fishermen*, HMSO, Scottish Home Dept.)

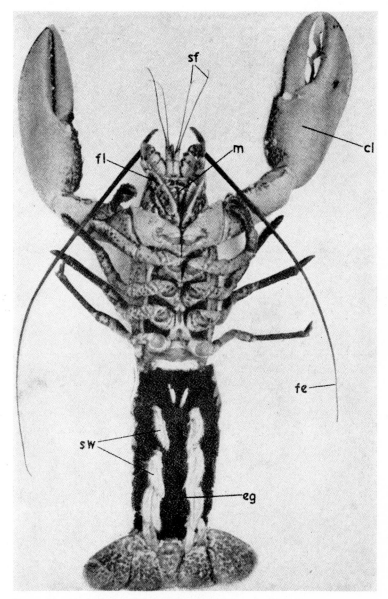

PLATE X. Female Berried Lobster—Underside: cl—big claw; eg—eggs or spawn; fe—long feelers; fl—feeding leg; m—mouth; sf—small feelers; sw—swimmerets or paddles
(From *Practical Hints for Lobster Fishermen*, HMSO Scottish Home Dept.)

PLATE XI.   French type crawfish pot. "Easy come, easy go . . .
undoubtedly the best"

PLATE XII.   Modern folding lobster and prawn creels are compact and easy to
handle and stow

However good the grounds are, though, this method is not satisfactory close inshore, as severe water movement may well tangle them into an unliftable snarl.

Pots are set on a leader or back rope of 2 in. circumference. To this each pot is hitched by its double $1\frac{1}{2}$ in. cir. rope, at intervals of about five fathoms. One end of the back rope is connected to an anchor and buoy or dahn rope, the length of which is dependent upon the depth of water. First over is the buoyed anchor, followed by the weighted pots, and another anchor and buoyed rope at the far end (Fig. 5). It is advisable not to set the fleet against the tide but with it and slightly across it, as this helps to carry the hitched pots clear of the back rope. Great care should be taken, however, to prevent the ropes from fouling the propeller, otherwise there could be severe trouble.

Mechanical hauling can be done against the tide. After the buoy and anchor are recovered, the back rope is led, through a universal roller well ahead of the beam, aft to the capstan position. As each pot comes aboard, it is unhitched and the back rope coiled down, preferably into a box. Alternatively, to avoid unhitching, the pot can remain attached to the back rope, but extreme care is necessary to avoid a snarl-up when re-setting, otherwise the setter might well get caught up and follow the fleet downwards. It is wise therefore to have thighboots of a size that are easily kicked off. As mine were on the tight side, the boxed back rope system was adhered to.

If this method is extensively used the best fishing team is made up of a crew of three. Number one looks after the hauling, number two clears the catch and re-baits, and number three attends to the capstan and coils down ready for shooting. By this method, several hundred pots can be fished in reasonable comfort and the cost of the extra man or boy is easily paid for.

There are many designs of capstan, both manufactured and home made. In my early days when I worked with Twm, we used what he aptly described as "Armstrongs' Patent", which was slowly efficient but very back-breaking. Years later, I made up an engine driven capstan consisting of the "gubbins" of a Bedford lorry steering, welded into an oil-tight supporting box of $\frac{1}{8}$ in. plate. The capstan head was turned up from a block of lignum vitae which lasts indefinitely. The drive was my belt and jockey pulley hitched to the fore end of the Kelvin Ricardo

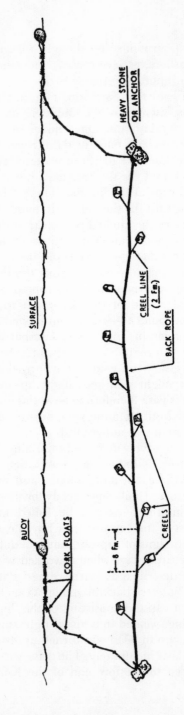

Fig. 5. Diagram of creels set in fleet of ten. (From *Practical Hints for Lobster Fishermen*, HMSO Scottish Home Dept.)

engine. This mock-up gave spartan service for several years and as far as I know is still working in another boat. All went well for some years, but as I was working single-handed it was necessary to haul beam on. It would of course, have worked much more easily further forward, but it was impossible to transfer the power lead.

Alan Smallwood—of later hydraulic winch fame—came up with the idea of using hydraulics. We hunted around lorry scrap yards and found a discarded hydraulic pump and motor,

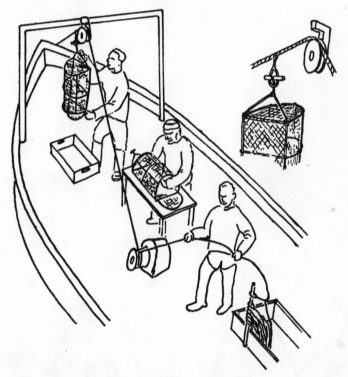

FIG. 6. " . . . a low goal-post affair placed well forward" is the best position for this type of winch

borrowed the local blacksmith's welding gear, and in due course produced a queer looking but efficient article that could be placed literally anywhere, due to the fact that the compressed oil could be piped to any position, from keelson to mast truck.

The best position for this winch, though I didn't try it, would have been hanging in a low goal-post affair placed well forward similar to Bob Leakey's excellent snatch block (Fig. 6 and Plate XVII).

Light Attraction

A good deal has been written and proved about this as far as fish are concerned, and although it is known that lobsters are shade lovers, it was decided to try out the idea. Several battery cells terminating in a flashlight bulb were wired up to one of the pots referred to above. Wiring and batteries were insulated by dipping in hot pitch, and the baited pot was set. At first light the next morning, about a dozen sizeable wrasse were found. The following night the bait was removed and the pot re-set with light. When raised, it was found to contain several wrasse and one of the largest soles I have come across. Though the pot was on good lobster ground the light most certainly did not attract them. To double check, the pot had its electrics removed, was baited and set in the same location, with the result that next morning it held two lobsters.

In 1958, Mr. A. C. Simpson of the Fisheries Laboratory at Lowestoft came up to Cardigan Bay with his team and gear and

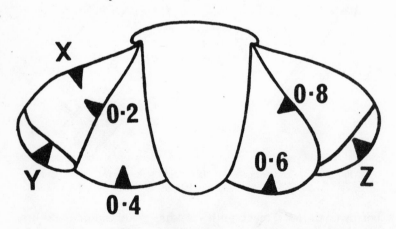

Fig. 7. Gibson's method of tail-punching to a code. "If marked at X, and 0.8, the lobster had a carapace length of 7.8 cm. If punched at Y and Z the carapace was 11.0 cm. in length." (From *Measurements and Growth of Irish Lobsters* by F. A. Gibson)

did a most useful, practical job of research into the lobster fisheries in this locality.

The object of the exercise was to test the catchability of several types of traditional pots, also to mark to a code and return all catches. There was a subsequent reward for all information relating to movement, shell-shedding and growth, and the point of pick-up. The reason for the latter was that as each dropping point was charted, a check could be kept on their wanderings. Subsequent movement, if any, seemed to be in a northerly direction and limited to two miles.

Mr. Simpson's marking method, the first time I had seen it done, was to tail-punch any of the five tail flippers with a 3/16th mark, which lasted for up to three shell-sheddings. The marks were to a strict code, which gave him the required information on recovery. (See Gibson's method, Fig. 7.)

Prior to this idea, plastic tags were fixed to the clippers—and of course were lost when the lobster shed its shell.

My own method was similar, in that I tried tagging immatures, softies and spawning hens with a twist of coloured plastic wire. Again, these were lost when shell-shedding occurred, but the information I gleaned convinced me that lobsters, wherever dropped, remained in the same location and did not travel very much.

Later, when I turned over to the tail punching idea, I proved one thing to my entire satisfaction, and that was that it is nothing short of criminal to retain immatures. Those just under nine inches increase their size to marketable proportions in just about a year, and the person who destroys or keeps them is a downright fool.

To me the most interesting experiment of the Simpson exercise was the testing of the catchability of various types of pots employed throughout the British fishery.

Simpson's method was to hitch half a dozen different types, all baited with gurnard, on to the same fleet. All types were traditional, and ranged from Welsh "football" to East Coasters of various designs and sizes.

The result was that the East Coaster emerged as the most efficient of the lot, and one particular design with a bigger floor area and increased height which is used off Llandudno topped the test, proving that the bigger the pot, the better it caught. As far as I know no parlour pots were tested, but a local lobsterman came up with the idea of netting off the upper storey of this outsize East Coaster with an easy in-leading cod end.

This proved so successful, that since then he has refused to use any other type, and invariably finds his catches holed up on the "bedroom floor".

Water Temperature

One thing, of which we knew little, that the Simpson exercise taught us was that water temperature is a most important factor in the early spring fishery. Apparently, lobsters do not start to search for more solid food, as offered by the baited pot, until the water has reached, or slightly topped, 50°F., or 10°C. Since learning this, a thermometer has become part of my standard equipment.

Each year I have kept a few early pots down and catches have proved to be minimal until the water was warmed up to the required temperature, which certainly bears out Dr. Simpson's theory. On checking my records I have noticed that the date is becoming steadily later.

It is indeed extraordinary how the old fishermen were governed by signs that now appear to have had some scientific basis. My friend Twm would never put his pots into the water until the farmer's corn was in the ear; in other words, by the time that happened, the water was about 50°F.

Although these days, the water seems to take longer to warm up in the spring, the catching season remains the same, for the movement and feeding cycle extends a like period into the autumn along the Welsh coast, and a late start is thus balanced by a late finish.

Chapter 7

More About Storing

HAD I known earlier what I now know about obtaining high winter prices, I would most certainly have built a sea pond and kept back the fittest lobsters caught when the summer flush knocked prices to rock bottom.

By fittest I mean hard-shelled, lively lobsters up to 2 lb. in weight. It would be useless to try to keep "sleepies" and large specimens, as heavy losses during storage always result from these categories.

The East coast Canadian and American scientists have done a good deal of work on long- and short-term storage and on our side of the Atlantic, Dr. H. J. Thomas of the Scottish Home Department has most usefully written his findings into a publication entitled "Lobster Storage". It can be obtained from H.M.S.O., Edinburgh. From this publication, which is a mine of information and which will prove most useful to lobstermen or merchants with ideas of storage, I have extracted a few of his findings.

Purity of Water

Pure water can frequently be achieved even in close proximity to towns. In the case of shore-based installations, near towns or harbours, great care must be taken. Water intakes must be arranged to allow neither surface, nor bottom water to be taken into the system.

It would, however, be advisable to ask the Ministry or the local Sea Fisheries Committee to carry out a pollution survey before embarking on construction. In open sea conditions, of course, this would be unnecessary.

When concrete is used, it is advisable to use some water-proofing compound in the mix to ensure water retention. Care should be taken to finish off floor and sides smoothly and allow for fall to water exits. This will facilitate occasional scrubbing out, and, if necessary, disinfecting. A smooth bottom will also lessen abrasion to shells, particularly the underside of claws. Avoid anything in the way of copper or brass in the installation, as these metals are highly toxic to lobsters.

For piping, black polythene has been successfully used, with stainless steel valves. Transparent piping has been found to encourage growth of algae.

Water Conditions

The salinity of sea water around the British Isles, away from estuaries, is between 30 and 35 per 1000 by weight. Lobsters can withstand dilutions, but this will depend on a reduced temperature and plenty of oxygen. Sites where salinity drops below 25 per 1000 should be avoided to prevent heavily diluted water from entering. As fresh water, in estuaries or other places where land water enters the sea, floats surfacewards, it is possible to draw water of the correct salinity from 3 ft. below the surface.

Water temperature off the British coast varies from 40°F. in February to 60° in August. Lobsters are capable of survival up to 80°F. if not in crowded conditions, but generally speaking tank temperatures should not rise above 65°F. Where possible, in shore-based installations fresh sea water is drawn continuously, passing through the system and flowing to waste. The rate of flow is kept in relation to the number of lobsters stored, and is maintained at a level to ensure adequate oxygen supplies, one gallon of water per lobster of $1\frac{1}{2}$ lb. should suffice. At 60°F. a flow of not less than one gallon per lobster per hour should suffice. Under these conditions there is a real advantage in shallow tanks as they are cheaper to build. Aeration is improved by having fairly high inlet pipes. If circulation is only occasional, six gallons per lobster will be required which can be helped by increasing the depth of water in the tank.

Aeration

The aeration system connected to a compressor and distributing pipes is sometimes used on circulating systems. The volume of air is more important than pressure. At times when there is no circulation, volume of air must be generous so that water is agitated. Aeration is better used to supplement re-circulation to sea rather than as an alternative.

One most important point in the construction of circulation tanks is that they be adequately roofed, as the lobster is a shade-loving animal. Roofing which excludes the direct rays of the sun helps to keep temperature down and discourages growth of algae.

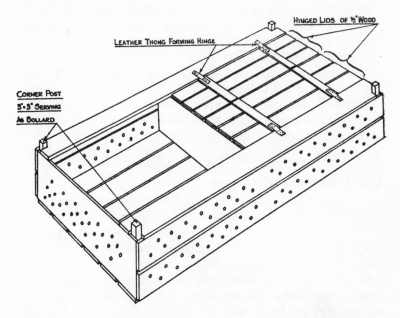

FIG. 8. Diagram of Large Twin Compartment Storage Box. The overall size is 12 feet × 6 feet × 2 feet. (From *Practical Hints for Lobster Fishermen*, HMSO Scottish Home Dept.)

Lobsters are Cannibals

If their claws are not immobilized, lobsters may fight to the death, especially if they are strangers, though I have known several lobsters in the same pot to live in perfect amity for some weeks. This was when a method of preventing escape from a parlour pot was being tried out.

Claws can be put out of action by tying with strong string or securing with rubber bands (rings cut from an old cycle tyre inner tube are also used). Personally I don't like any of these methods, as there is a high rot element involved. The Americans may have the answer in their use of rot-proof elasticated bands.

Anything is preferable to the small wooden wedges they used to drive into the soft hind joint on top of the thumb. This must have given the animal absolute hell. It also rotted the claw flesh.

After a few lessons from a French lobsterman, I perfected the sinew-dislocating method. A very thin blade, such as that on a ground-down vegetable knife, is inserted into the soft thumb joint to less than half-an-inch and gently raised until the faintest of clicks is felt. This renders the thumb loose and useless, with the minimum of discomfort to the lobster. Care must be taken not to let the knife go too deep, otherwise the lobster will throw the claw off at the shoulder.

Although the claw mechanism comes back into use after a few weeks, I have kept lobsters which have been immobilised in this way living in perfect harmony for six months.

Other Methods of Storage

Sea ponds and circulation tanks are for the catch collecting merchant, or for co-operatives. The usual method adopted by lone lobstermen is to store their catch in moored box-like rafts, or in sunken cages (Fig. 8). I abandoned the raft type after one containing five hundredweight of lobsters was lost in an onshore gale, and when I switched to the bottom-hugging cages, lobster deaths were reduced to almost nil. No doubt the higher death rate of the former method was due to the fact that the rafts became too warm as they floated near the surface.

On one occasion we caught a number of lobsters with tied claws. There was nothing peculiar in this as they had obviously been lost after having been caught, but what was peculiar was the method of tying. As far as we could tell, they had not been tied on the Welsh coast, so we came to the conclusion that an Irish keeping raft had gone adrift, come over on the prevailing winds and tide and broken open on our doorstep. The tied method was identical to that used years ago by my old master, Irish Twm, and consisted of two round turns of tarred twine, with ends knotted and tucked under for safety.

To digress. On completion of my apprenticeship to Twm, he decided to go on his pension, and only fish for a bit of "baccy money". Within a couple of weeks, he was dead. Returning from a celebratory visit to the village pub one dark and stormy night, he put on a bit too much starboard helm and staggered off the cliff path into a fifty foot deep rocky-bottomed tidal blow-hole known as "The Pot". The post-mortem revealed that the fall had broken his neck. There was no water in his lungs, which was indeed fortunate for this indicated that he was spared the horror of drowning on the incoming tide.

Chapter 8

Hibernian Sandwich

I RECENTLY did a tour of enquiry along the southern and western coasts of Ireland, where in addition to many other things, including taking in large quantities of draught stout, I learned much about the storage of lobsters at Yann Mauger's colossal sea pond and shore installation in Connemara. It could, he told me, deal with up to 300 tons of lobsters when full.

This trip materialised because I thought the best way to learn about crawfish, of which I had not the least knowledge, was to go and see Burdon-Jones, Ph.D., who heads the Marine Biology Station at Menai Bridge, Anglesey. As it turned out, however, crawfish weren't his strong point either! But he came up with the very bright idea of my going over to Dublin and making my number with Alec Gibson, Ph.D., kingpin of shellfish (with the accent on crawfish) for the Irish Dept. of Fisheries.

My record of that visit was published in *Fishing News* and I give here a few extracts:

Dr. Burdon-Jones' suggestion gave me the excuse to do something I had wanted to do for many years—meet up with Irish inshoremen, preferably in quayside pubs, and sort out the history of my forebears—a rebellious lot. This had been an impossibility in the past, as during the fishing season I had been tied to my pot lines.

My first call was on Dr. Gibson at his headquarters in Dublin where I was received with outstanding courtesy and his smoothing of my future travels with introductions to many interesting people in the trade, along the southern and western seaboard.

Dr. Gibson told me that in his opinion the western side was very under-fished from the shellfish viewpoint. In this I was later wholeheartedly to agree with him when I visited the many, repeat many, west-facing superbly built but deserted quaysides (Fig. 9).

The trouble of course is de-population, by the lure of high and fairly easy-come-by wages "across the water". In the coastal districts few youngsters above school-leaving age are to be found. A very deserted countryside it is, and one can drive many miles without seeing a soul. Not once did I see a bent back in a field but plenty of good looking young beef and mutton grazing at will over the deserted crofts. Transport in spite of superb roads, seems to be limited to that attractive little animal, the donkey.

From Dublin, I drove due south to the once-flourishing fishing port of Kinsale but found the accent there was on big game fishing for the tourist, although there were still a few smallish trawlers and lobster boats working seawards. Even an

FIG. 9. Kilmakilloge Harbour on the Kenmare estuary. One of the many deserted fishing ports along the West Coast of Ireland

up-to-date fish cannery had just closed down for shortage of raw materials.

Next day I was off towards the west to look up Mr. John Wycherly, who, Alec Gibson told me, had one of the best informed brains in the shellfish business. I found the Wycherly set-up a model of efficiency—banks of continuous circulation roofed-in tanks for lobsters and crawfish (Plates XX and XXI show similar installations), two deep-freeze chambers for what he called prawns but are more generally known as Norwegian lobsters or scampi.

I was indeed intrigued by their preparation, especially the

small ones, no bigger than an over-sized shrimp. In a surgically clean "operation theatre" three small boys, presumably of the Wycherly clan, were having a whale of a time de-heading and jamming their backsides—the prawns backsides that is—against a hollow copper needle. Then with the touch of a foot-pedal a "ping" of compressed air was released which blew the meat into a hopper.

John told me that he was unable to get enough prawns to keep his plant going so had decided to go out and drag the mud on his own account. With this in mind, he was daily awaiting delivery from Sweden of a specially-designed boat.

The only pot that interests the Irish lobstermen is the French type, excellent for crawfish but not so clever with lobsters. I can quite see their viewpoint, as the traditional spouts are too narrow for crawfish whereas they have no trouble in falling into the very wide spout of the barrel-like wood-slatted pots from France.

It is the slat that does the damage. Too widely spaced for lobster, it is possible for them to get a clipper through and when these rather lightly stone-weighted pots start to roll about the bottom, the jammed claw is torn off. The French pot tends to catch the larger lobsters, which are not so popular on the market. Prices for primes—by primes I mean up to 2 lb. in weight, ex-boat—ranged from 10s. in the south and east to 7s. up in Connemara. This was in early June 1965. Larger ones and one-armed unfortunates attracted about 1s. less.

Talking of these cripples, Alec Gibson told me of an interesting weight comparison. He had carefully weighed two of the same size, ex-pot, one having two clippers and the other only one. Weights were nearly identical, proving a hefty intake of water through the wound. The weight remained constant until the wound had healed and a new claw had started to grow. Then the weight dropped back. Lobstermen, please note.

Poking around John Wycherly's deep freeze, where my feet froze to the floor, I saw a number of rock-hard lobsters. These according to John were "sleepies", otherwise those that do not travel well from boat to plant. The interesting point is that even after a freeze-up of several months, so I was told, they lose none of their pristine glories or flavour when cooked, but I would like to check this point for myself.

Onwards towards Castleton-Bearhaven. Here I found a busy

quayside with a number of 60-ft. trawlers working by the day and landing very mixed though reasonably heavy catches. There were also several motorised lobster boats up to 30 ft. in length, and as far as I gathered, a tidal lobster pond that was not meeting with much success.

On my way to this port, I dropped off at Bantry to drink to a long-dead man. He was a forebear of mine who collected a baronetcy for doing an all-time record cross-country ride to Cork to call out the military to deal with the invading French when they landed at Bantry Bay at the end of the seventeen hundreds. History relates that he had a girl friend in the town of Cork, so it may be assumed that fear plus love spurred him on.

I had every intention of visiting Mr. H. Mills who has a large sea keeping-pond between Goleen and Crookhaven, but due to faulty map-reading, I found we were travelling north. I made a valiant attempt to traverse a left-turn, but ended up on one of the many limbs of land, and as night was overtaking us, had to turn back in search of a lodging.

This fishery near Crookhaven was mainly concerned with crawfish, and I was told that the French sent a boat, fitted with circulation tanks, over every week or so to remove the catch. Following the sea edge to the north, we visited port after port, mostly deserted but still in excellent condition.

Seawards in every case looked marvellous lobster and crawfish country. There is little doubt that this western coast is very under-fished and I think there is a great opportunity for some adventurous young men from our overfished areas to set up shop, providing they brought along with them know-how and equipment. The Fisheries Department would, I feel sure, welcome them, as long as they set up business in one of the derelict ports to the north or south.

This idea was sold very hard to me by several shellfish merchants who, in their own interests, were doing their utmost to encourage the fishery. Near Clifden, I met a great character called Marteen Michael. He was 80 years of age, with a width of a stable door and of a height that entirely dwarfed my six feet two. He had spent his life crofting and lobstering until he took up seaweed gathering. The type he was after was a ribbon-like weed of immense length which grew well below low springs and had to be scythed off the bottom from his curragh, and retrieved

88

spaghetti-like, with a long fork—a job for a superbly strong man.
He did not know what the processors made of it, but volun-
teered: "They are after making so many things with it in
Liverpool that they won't be telling you."

From what Marteen told me, he was not a big eating man.
He admitted to tea and bread-and-butter for most meals, with
perhaps a couple of eggs on reaching home in the evenings. The
secret of his immense frame, I learned later, was his intake of
draught porter. In his younger days, especially on fair days, he
was a four-and-twenty pint man and at closing time challenged
the whole of Connemara to do battle.

FIG. 10.   Eighteen foot canvas covered Irish fishing 'curragh'.
"Floats on the dew and is a marvellous sea-keeper"

There seemed to be very few sizeable boats in the west and
seagoing boats were limited to the curragh (pronounced
"currock") (Fig. 10). Eighteen to twenty feet long with a beam
of about 5 ft., they are propelled by three pairs of so-called oars,
which to me looked like rowing sticks with the tiniest of blades.
The hull is constructed of stretched, tarred flaxen canvas.
Timbers are of grown sticks as thick as your thumb, fastened—
presumably for economy—with galvanised wire nails. Between
canvas and timbers are wafer-thin planks running full length.
Their draught is so light that they might well float on the dew.

I found these feather-light hulls, with their through-tholepin rowing sticks, delightfully easy to pull. But because of their high prows they proved to be the devil—in my unskilled hands—to directionally control in a cross-breeze.

My last call was near Cleggan in Connemara. It was on Alec Gibson's list as an absolute "must" and turned out to be quite a large sea inlet, walled and partitioned off in high concrete compartments (Fig. 11). It had room for 300 tons of lobsters and crawfish and was huge in comparison with John Wycherly's circulation installation which was limited (at that time) to 30 tons. This colossal outfit was owned and run by Mr. Yann

Fig. 11.   Lobster and crawfish seaponds at Cleggan, Connemara, with a capacity of 300 tons

Mauger, a Breton who got into trouble with the post-war French Government for heading a movement connected with Freedom from France for Brittany. He escaped to England and landed a Lectureship at a Welsh University. But not for long. The Central Government applied for his extradition so he departed to the freedom of the Irish Free State where he joined another Breton who had started the Connemara installation in 1922.

When I saw it at the beginning of June it was undergoing a spring-clean and the work team were building queer-looking shelters on the bottom of the lobster pound. These consisted of little hides or houses, about 12 in. high, of rough stone, topped with a few slats of wood held in place with other stones. Apparently, the lobsters used these hides as sunshades and spent most of the time under their cover.

Mauger told me that it was not necessary to house the crawfish like this, as they had the good sense to dodge sunlight by following the wall shadows around. I gathered the idea was to store shell-fish during the summer glut and supply the Continental market during the higher-priced winter months. As required, they were taken out of the main ponds, transferred to sea-water circulation tanks ashore and given a good fizzing up with air-produced oxygen prior to being nestled in wood wool and packed into cardboard cartons, in readiness for their journey by air.

A sideline experiment was in progress. In the pool shallows there were wooden trays carrying an assortment of oyster spat and, from what I saw of the various states of development, the finished product seemed to be a highly marketable commodity.

Yann told me about his feeding arrangements in the sea pond. He agrees with me that feeding under longish term sea pond storage is unnecessary. The only time he fed was when his lodgers got on the rampage and started to chase each other around with murder in their hearts. To stop this he scattered a barrowful of crushed mussels into the lobster pond. He gave me one rather surprising piece of information. Whereas the lobsters could not open the mussels, the crawfish had no difficulty in doing so, with their tiny clippers.

Prices, ex-boat, in Connemara were a shilling or so below the south coast, but even at this price, Mauger thought, crawfish would shortly be over-valued from the export viewpoint. Supplies of frozen tails coming from south of the Equator were finding a ready and competitive sale on the European market.

Lobsters, he thought, would always be in good demand, due to their limited range to the southward. As far as I know only odd ones are taken beyond the limits of the Bay of Biscay. Another interesting point I gathered was that, due to misunder-standings of descriptions of lobsters, crawfish and Norwegian lobsters that had arisen on consignment notes going foreign, the Latin names were exclusively used. This, indeed, seemed good sense.

Queerly enough—it must be inbred—I share the Irish fisher-man's dislike of dealing with crabs, and he, like me, seems to bash them on the gunwale and drop them over the side unless the crushed body is used for bait.

Dr. Gibson told me that there were some really excellent crab grounds and a ready market in Ireland, but so far he had failed to convert the men to this fishery. He is treating the matter so seriously, that he is putting on a scientist to try to convince the catchers that there is good money in crabs. Good luck to him. Fashions take a long time dying—especially in Ireland.

I found that in Ireland, even in these days—outside the cities, that is—there was a total absence of rat-race. In the far west the donkey for transport is still paramount. There I learned the body-building elements of tea brewed the day before, home-made bread and porter by the pint.

Chapter 9

About the Crab

A s I have said before, I have rather a "thing" about crabs in the raw. I do, however, put the accent on "raw". In my opinion, subject of course, to correct preparation, they knock a lobster for six flavourwise.

The "thing" no doubt has its roots in the fact that both Twm and his wife each lost a finger to the bone-destroying claws of crabs. If a crab gets a hold of any sort, the only way to deal with it is to immediately crush it underfoot. Even then, it may be too late. The lobster bite is an on-and-off affair, and usually, at worst a bloody business. This can be minimised by quickly tearing the offending claw off. It is impossible to do this to a crab.

Another point against crabs as far as we are concerned, is that there is a minimal local market, and our storage facilities being laid out for lobsters, the catch was not large enough to warrant keeping for dispatch to inland markets.

Although, with a little practice, it is possible to be sure of a lobster's marketable condition by the feel of the carapace, which should be hard, the same does not apply to the crab. I have, however, learned the art of selection from professional crabbers, and tips have ranged from shaking them alongside your ear and listening for water, to cooking them.

Providing there is no water to be heard, and that the shell or box is not too clean and highly coloured—indicating recent shedding—also that the walking legs are strong and springy, you will be on fairly sound marketing ground.

It is as well to test these theories by simmer-cooking a random few in sea water for about twenty minutes. They should be placed in cold water and brought to the boil as they are inclined to cast their claws on sudden immersion in hot. When cooked, open the box and if reasonably full and the lining is of a reddish brown colour and fairly solid, the rest of your market selection should be fit for sale.

If, on the other hand, the box is only half full and the contents grey-green and sloppy, it is a waste of time trying to market them. With experience, it is possible to be fairly sure by feel and look to decide on their condition.

Incidentally, another method of cooking recommended by the Torry Research Station is to first kill the crab by spiking it through the eye, and then to boil it in a 2-3 per cent salt solution for 20-30 minutes, depending on size.

My personal feeling is that my way is the more humane of the two, for the gradually warming water more or less anaesthetizes the crab and it is likely it knows very little about what is happening.

Reproduction

Here I must quote the scientists and do so from Leaflet No. 4, obtainable from the Secretary, Dept. of Lands, Fisheries Division, Dublin.

"Edible crabs abound in sandy patches and rocky weed-strewn areas in water depths varying from a few to over 30 fathoms. Whilst crabs may be captured at all times of the year, their suitability for market at any particular time will be governed by the condition of their reproductive organs. Normally, if the reproductive organs are well developed, the meat of the crab will be in good condition. Reproduction in crabs varies greatly from place to place and year to year, but a generalised description of the reproductive cycle is as follows. Crabs spawn during the winter months, and in doing so migrate to deeper water, usually farther offshore. Once they have spawned, their edible parts are in very poor condition, and the meat content is very low. At this stage, they are commonly called 'black-sick' crabs. When spawning has ceased, crabs recommence to feed actively and move slowly from the deeper offshore waters to the shallower depths inshore where suitable feeding is found, normally in abundance. The jack-crabs (males) may reach the inshore waters earlier than the hen-crabs (females) and generally their rate of recovery from the effects of spawning is faster than that of the hen-crabs.

"In certain areas, there can, therefore, be a fishery primarily for jack-crabs during the late spring and early summer months. As summer progresses, so increasing numbers of hen-crabs reappear in inshore waters and ordinarily they are for the greater part in good condition by mid-July, reaching their best in the autumn months. On the whole, crab fisheries can normally be expected to reach their highest level of production in the autumn although the fishing season may extend from April to November. This being only a general synopsis of the behaviour and movements of crabs, it must be realised that considerable differences occur as between one locality and another under the influence of annually varying conditions.

"Crabs appear to be strongly affected by their environment and the type of feeding in it. For example, if summer climatic conditions inshore are sub-normal resulting in the return of the inwardly migrating stocks to unfavourable feeding grounds, their rate of recovery is drastically slowed and a reasonably good crab fishery may not become available until the late autumn or early winter months, in which case the inshore fishing grounds may have to be temporarily forsaken for those further offshore and in deeper water."

Shell Shedding

As with lobsters and shrimps, the growth of a crab is governed by periodic shedding of the shell. When the old shell has been dispensed with, the crab absorbs considerable quantities of water, and thus increases its size. The new shell gradually hardens and no further growth is possible until the next moult.

Again, this confirms the stupidity of the minority of fishermen, who keep immatures, as the increase in weight between sheddings can be considerable.

It has been found that the increase in size during moulting is similar for males and females, and varies from 20 to 30 per cent of the original shell width. On the other hand, the difference in weight between male and female is marked. On average, females double their weight after moulting, while males become two and a half times as heavy. Thus, a $4\frac{1}{2}$ in. female which weighs 8 oz. will, after only one moult, reach a size of $5\frac{3}{4}$ in. and will then weigh 16 oz. A further moult will increase her size to $6\frac{1}{2}$ in.

A male of the same original size and weighing $8\frac{1}{2}$ oz. will also moult to a size of $5\frac{3}{4}$ in., but will then tip the scales at 22 oz.

As with lobsters, experiments have been carried out to determine the movements and growth rates of crabs (Figs. 12 & 13), and one of the most successful ways of tagging them has been the "suture" method. This has the great advantage of remaining with the crab during the moult.

The tag is attached by wire or nylon through two holes pierced in the line of separation, which runs right round the body of the crab (Plate XXII). The shell opens along this line to allow the soft crab to emerge, and trials have shown that the tag in no way interferes with the process.

A 7-in. female crab tagged by the suture method was recently recaptured 140 miles to the north of the area of release at Sheringham, Norfolk. In just over six years it had grown two inches, and was estimated to be about ten years old.

One of the results of an experiment with this method of tagging carried out by the Ministry of Agriculture and Fisheries' Shellfish Research Laboratory during recent months has shown that on the east coast of Britain there is in progress a northerly migration of female crabs.

Fishing Methods

Generally speaking, the same fishing method applies to crab fishing as that already discussed in lobstering. Pots are similar in construction but are usually larger in body and spout dimensions. I have seen Cornish, French and East Coast types fished with approximately the same results. In my opinion the best of the lot was an oversized four-bowed East Coaster with two side spouts and an end compartment or "parlour" reached by a fairly wide-mouthed spout, which of course represents to the crab or lobster the easiest way "out". It has the advantage of being nearly escape-proof and can be left down for longer periods. It must, however, be admitted that the largest and most marketable jack crabs are taken in the wide-spouted French or Cornish types, but these "easy-come-easy-go" pots must be raised often; at a minimum, twice a day.

One most important point is the ballasting of pots—they must lie quietly on the bottom. As a rough guide, an East Coaster requires 14 lb. of concrete (run in wet). The French type of pot needs more, as the greater amount of timber used in its construction gives it more buoyancy.

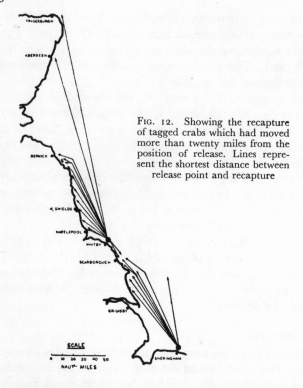

FIG. 12. Showing the recapture of tagged crabs which had moved more than twenty miles from the position of release. Lines represent the shortest distance between release point and recapture

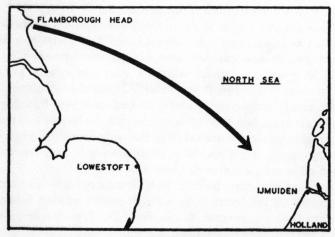

FIG. 13. The 170 mile track of a tagged female crab released off the Yorkshire coast by Burnham-on-Crouch scientists

Bait

Crabs do not seem to have the gentle touch of lobsters when dealing with bait, so it must be securely fastened. They are inclined to tear it away from its anchorage and lose it by tidal action operating steadily through the mesh and bars. When this happens, they begin to look for the way out, and if the pot is of the netted variety, they set about chewing and tearing their way through. This can be prevented to some extent if the bait is securely tied in netting, as this will hold the crab's interest for a much longer period. Although I have heard it argued to the contrary, my experience has been that for crabs the fresher the bait—anything, in fact, that has once lived—the better the pot catches. The only disadvantage in using some fresh bait is that it also attracts congers and dogfish. The reverse, as I have said, applies to lobsters.

Handling

A very useful list of "do's and don'ts" to bear in mind when dealing with crabs has been published by the Ministry of Technology and Torry Research Station, and it is worth recording here.

Handle crabs as little as possible after capture to minimise claw shedding, and for the same reason, never haul a crab from the pot by its claws.

Never leave crabs on an exposed deck. The wind and sun rapidly weaken them and this often results in a high death rate. They should preferably be stowed after catching, but in any event should immediately be boxed or put into the bottom of the boat.

To keep crabs alive for several days, pack them carefully into floating boxes which allow good water circulation, but ensure they have room to move and breathe.

Transporting live crabs inland can be done quite easily if certain rules are adhered to. Pack them closely, back uppermost in a ventilated box or barrel with a good pad of damp wood shavings in the bottom. It is essential to crowd them as this prevents any attempt on their part to start tribal wars. Before putting the lid on the barrel, allow it to stand for half an hour or so, as the crabs will shuffle down into a hardpacked mass, and it will then be possible to pack in more, prior to topping off with another pad of damp shavings.

If possible, transport them during the cool of the night hours to prevent casualties due to high daytime temperatures.

In this way, and by taking a little more care, the catch will arrive in excellent condition and will, as a result, fetch better prices.

Chapter 10

About the Crawfish

WHAT little I know about Crawfish—spelt with a "w" please —has been limited to fishing around the Mediterranean and the Canary Islands. In the Mediterranean they are mainly caught by both trawl and pot, although a few are taken in trammels and other bottom-hugging nets. The Canary inshoremen use a flat, circular contraption with a diameter of 6 ft. and a height of 1 ft. 6 in. This is built on a steel frame and is covered with wire netting and some of them, in addition to a side entrance, have another entrance on top. It also doubles as a fish trap.

Although some fourteen miles to the southward of my lobster beat there is a flourishing crawfishery, I have never caught one of these crustaceans, and assumed they just didn't inhabit my area. But there is always the unexpected.

Roy Midwinter, of skin diving fame (Plate XXIV), recently asked me to pin-point an old steamer wreck for him. I was able to do this with some accuracy as it is always good for a few lobsters. That they inhabit a metal wreck was evident, as their shells were invariably iron-moulded.

Roy found the wreck, now reduced and flattened to a conglomeration of steel sheets, in five fathoms, and to everyone's surprise brought up a sizeable crawfish and reported several others in the vicinity. I think the reason we had not caught them was due to the fact that we use East Coasters with netted covers and spouts, which bears out the theory that these spiny creatures avoid anything that might entangle them.

Had we been using French or Cornish types we might have caught some, though not in any quantity, for my old friend Twm always used large Cornish pots, and as far as I know, only ever caught one in the area.

To the best of my knowledge very little has been written about the practical side of the crawfishery in this country, and it is

99

good to know that Mr. Hepper of the Conway Shellfish Research Station has the job in hand.

I have, however, found a most informative, though rather alarming, paper issued by the Australian Fisheries Department, attractively written and illustrated for the use of their crawfishermen, and there is no reason to think that the information does not tally with crawfish and lobsters in the Northern Hemisphere. One thing that sticks out like a sore finger, is that the Department is desperately worried about the catastrophic downfall in stocks, to say nothing of the livelihood of the fishermen.

Australian catches have fallen from an average of six per pot hauled in 1948 to one per pot in 1964. It has a parallel in our own lobster fishery, as when I started lobstering, and pots, when weather allowed, were lifted twice daily, catches averaged nearly two per haul. Nowadays, one lobster for every second haul is considered good fishing, and the catch is still falling.

Something must obviously be done about this, and maybe the answer lies in artificial rearing from eggs and cosseting the young lobsters until they can look after themselves. If this is impracticable it may be necessary to close areas on a rota basis for a few years, otherwise it seems inevitable that catches will dribble to a near full-stop. At present there is a movement on foot amongst the Inshore Fishery Committees to investigate the possibility of altering their Bye-laws to cover, by licence, professional lobstermen. It would then knock out, the (at times) heavy landings of part time potters and divers. Salmon have been handled this way—why not lobsters and crawfish?

In this country the crawfish is not relished to the same extent as on the Continent, and until a few years ago, the British market was minimal. So much so, that French "crabbers" fishing up here in Cardigan Bay used to swop weight per weight in lobsters for crawfish with the Bardsey crofter-fishermen, who in addition to catching lobsters, were sitting on a crawfish mine in the deep and troubled waters surrounding their island.

To revert to our Australian friends, I think their observations are well-worth some space, and so I quote from Messrs. B. K. Bowen and R. G. Chittleborough's well-written but woeful tale of crawfish. They write:

"Each year, fishermen are removing vast numbers of crawfish

from the fishing grounds. If the industry is to continue at the high level it has reached, obviously much will depend on the capacity of the remaining crawfish to provide replacements and for these in turn to move on to the grounds and to grow to legal size. One of the most important tasks of fishery scientists, therefore, is to study and become thoroughly familiar with all aspects of the life-cycle of the crawfish.

"In recent years, we have collected quite a lot of information about the life-cycle that gives important pointers towards future conservation, research, and development possibilities."

Spawning

The female crawfish can mature at three to four years of age, although some take longer. At her last moult before breeding, groups of long fine hairs appear on the swimmerets on the undersurface of each tail segment. Mating takes place in winter with the male depositing a sperm packet, the "tar spot", on the undersurface of the female between her last pair of legs. Although almost equal numbers of males and females are present, we do not know whether one male serves more than one female.

Eggs are laid during the spring, the actual time probably varying with water temperature. More than 100,000 eggs may be laid at a time by one female, who, as far as we know, spawns every year. The eggs pass through a pair of openings at the base of the third pair of legs. At the same time, the action of the last pair of legs scraping the "tar spot" releases the sperm, which then fertilizes the eggs as they pass back to stick to the fine hairs on the swimmerets.

Following fertilization, the eggs are carried for about 10 weeks before the tiny larvae, or developing baby crawfish, are released in the latter part of summer. After release the larvae rise to the surface and are carried out to sea. For about a year these flattened, transparent larvae drift in the open ocean, feeding and growing.

When about a year old, and still almost transparent, the young crawfish return to the coast and settle on the bottom. They spend the next two or three years on the coastal reefs, growing steadily at each moult. At about 3 or 4 years of age they reach adolescence and many moult into the familiar "white" stage

and move out to deeper water, where they gradually darken again. Not all craws go through this "white" stage, however.

From hereon, maturity is reached, breeding commences, and the whole cycle starts again. Growth of mature crawfish is generally much slower, although the "jumbo" size male may not be especially old. It could be that his growth rate did not slow down like the others. We do notice, however, that females do not grow as large as males.

One interesting sidelight on crawfish that many fishermen have observed is the tendency of this species to drop legs when they are frightened. Some think this may serve to decoy an enemy who will stay to chew the legs left behind. We have observed that at moulting, crawfish replace the lost legs with complete, but slightly smaller, new ones. One specimen observed in the aquarium grew eight new legs at one moult, although as a result of such effort it did not grow any larger at that moult.

Of necessity we have had to paint a grim picture of declining crawfish numbers and of the real threat to the livelihood of fishermen and their families. Furthermore, we have stressed that there are NO prospects of increasing the total annual catch until, through research, we have learnt more about the numerous problems involved.

The first step must be to stabilise the present catch. It is a poor outlook for fishermen, who work hard to take a reasonable catch, only to be faced with fewer and fewer crawfish in their pots each year. A steady catch, ensuring stable incomes for fishermen and a regular flow of fish for processors, is most desirable.

There are two ways of stabilizing and increasing recruitment, both of which require long-term planning—management of natural stocks and artificial hatching and rearing.

As we now depend almost entirely on the growth and entry of young crawfish into the fishable stock to keep up the catch, we must investigate all possible methods of protecting these juveniles. Naturally, a large number of undersize crawfish enter pots and traps and many are brought to the surface. Even if all of these are thrown back, some will die of damage or weakening in handling, and others because of exposure to natural enemies, while seeking fresh shelter. We have observed, for example, that craws returned immediately to the water appear dazed and confused and become easy prey to predators.

The best way to protect young crawfish is not to bring them to the surface at all. Escape gaps in the traps or pots allow the undersize craws to escape before reaching the surface. Recent tests by the Western Australian Department of Fisheries and Fauna have shown that crawfish seek to escape from pots soon after feeding. Because of this, those that can pass through gaps usually do so long before the pot is pulled.

The tests also showed that gaps up to 2⅛-in. width do not reduce the catch of legal-size crawfish, but allow most of those undersize to escape. However, some just at legal size can be pushed through gaps of this width. On the other hand, a 2-in. × 1-in. gap retains all marketable crawfish in the pot, yet still allows many of the undersize to escape.

Of the 100,000 or more eggs hatched by each female, only about 30 ever return from the ocean phase of their life-cycle. This very high rate of loss suggests a possible line of attack on the problem of increasing crawfish numbers. Perhaps the young larvae could be cultured in tanks and released on the reefs when ready to settle. Some fishermen have talked also of holding undersize crawfish in feeding ponds until large enough to harvest.

This, as anyone will agree, is food for thought, and I think should be considered very seriously by those involved in our own lobster and crawfishing industry.

The demand for shellfish has increased considerably in recent years and will probably continue to do so, but unless something practical is done—and soon—fishermen are going to drift away from what is, after all, a precarious living.

Experiments in rearing plaice under artificial conditions in the Isle of Man and elsewhere appear to be proving successful, and it should be possible, as suggested, to rear lobsters and crawfish successfully until they are of a size to be able to fend for themselves in their natural conditions. By this method, a valuable industry can be rejuvenated.

The question is, however, who is going to take the first step, and more important, will their investment be protected by means of licensing *bone fide* lobster and crawfishermen?

Chapter 11

Useful Tips on Line Fishing

THERE are so many excellent books available on the fishing rod side of the sport, including A. E. Cooper's "Sea Fishing", that I will stick to the more resultful "pot and profit" side. I have used, with varying luck, the following methods, but first let us have a look at our quarry and its haunts. About October, fish, with certain exceptions, leave the cooling inshore waters in the Northern Hemisphere, go deep to winter quarters, and start returning about March for spawning. It is impossible to lay down any hard and fast rule, as their arrival and departure varies from district to district.

Cod. This fish runs up to 100 lb. in weight but it is more likely to be taken in codling form. It's lateral line is white, and follows the curve of the back and its colour is greeny-grey above and white below. Baits, and this goes for most inshore fish, are worms, mussels, soft crab, immature fish or pieces cut off larger ones, with the accent on very fresh herring.

Whiting. A delightful dish if cooked properly. It lends itself to smoking and is so table-worthy that it is known as the "chicken of the sea". In colour it is lighter and more silvery than the cod, and has a light brown lateral line, but unlike the cod and haddock, it has no under-chin barbule.

Haddock. Average 16 inches in length and is easily identified by black marks either side of the forrard fin. At its best when smoked.

Skate. Though there is little resemblance, it is related to the dogfish family. Average weight 10 lb. but some grow on and top the 100 lb. mark. Most attractive bait is a piece of mackerel or herring.

Plaice. Average length 14 inches. Top side brownish grey with orange spots. Underside white. Has a preference for worm or mussel bait, which goes for flat fish generally.

Flounder. Top side brown to black. Underside white, its

PLATE XIII.   Two types of pot were experimented with including this expensive
one, but it gave no better results than the traditional East Coaster

PLATE XIV.   This is the inkwell type of pot made of willow at Port Clais, being
used in Ramsey Sound. (From *The Lobster Fishery of Wales*, by A. C. Simpson,
HMSO Fishery Investigations)

PLATE XV. Spherical Pots at Porth Merediog, Aberdaron
(From *The Lobster Fishery of Wales*, HMSO)

PLATE XVI. The American Parlour Pot

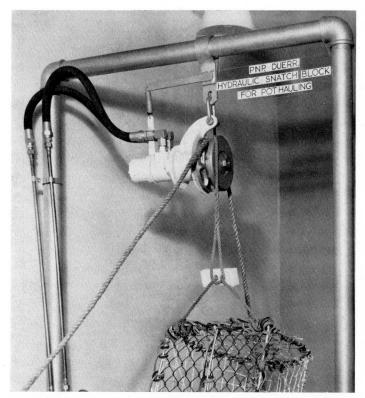

PLATE XVII.   Hydraulic Snatch block used to reduce heavy work hauling pots.

Photo: Roy Midwinter

PLATE XVIII.   Spanish type keep basket placed at a depth of 50 feet

108

PLATE XIX. The Lobster and the Beatle (see large claw)

PLATE XX. An effective lobster tank for storing lobsters at Berwick on Tweed.
The water is kept at a constant 50°F by refrigeration and losses have been largely
eliminated.

PLATE XXI. Selecting lobsters for market from an emptied pool.

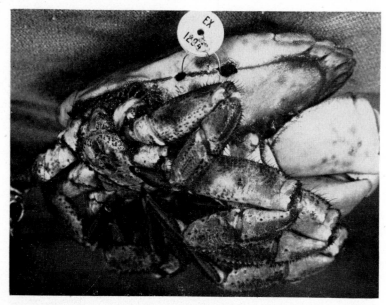

PLATE XXII. The "suture" method of tagging crabs to trace their movement and rates of growth

PLATE XXIII. At Portmadoc, Michael Byrne prepares a bag of mussels for despatch to Billingsgate

Photo: Roy Midwinter

PLATE XXIV. Divers seeking crawfish at a depth of 110 feet

PLATE XXV. "Scampi" or Nephrops prawns shown on Leakey prawn creels—
note size of matchbox.

PLATE XXVI. Prawn traps set off Skye caught (some years back) at least £1 a
week for *Sweet Home* fishing vessel.

length averages 12 inches. If caught in brackish water the flesh has an insipid taste.

Witch. Top side brown, underside grubby white. Lateral line almost straight. Prefers deeper water and a crustacean diet.

Several Varieties

Mullet. There are several varieties in our waters, the most common being the grey, which is identifiable by large scales and a tiny mouth. It has an average weight of 2 lb. and is coloured blue-grey on top and silvery below. It is seldom caught on lines, as its diet consists mostly of weeds and the edible contents of mud. On the south coast it is taken, in season, in immense quantities with a beach seine net.

Bass. Similar in colour to the mullet, but has smaller scales; its average weight 2 lb. When on the feed it takes practically any bait but at other times may be teased and taken with spinning gear. Care must be taken in handling as they have a murderously spiky dorsal fin.

Wrasse. A most colourful fish, ranging from greeny-brown to gold. It lives among seaweed and rocks and takes practically any bait. Due to its multiplicity of bones it is not table-worthy, but makes an excellent soup. Buried for a few days it stands "high", and is most attractive as a lobster pot bait.

Conger. Needs no description. Runs in length up to 9 feet and can weigh up to 200 lb. Feeds nocturnally unless the water is deep. Fish of almost any sort can be used as bait, but it must be absolutely fresh. They are reputed to bark and sometimes snap when landed, but although I have been shipmates with hundreds of them I have never heard or seen this happen. Any size can be instantaneously killed by piercing the spine directly behind the head with a bradawl.

Gurnard. Many varieties, with colour ranging from grey to shrimp pink. They are bottom feeders and take both bait and lure. Due to its outer armour it makes an excellent lobster pot bait. Skinned and fried it is most delicious.

Pollack and Saithe. Although similar in shape, size and rocky haunt to the pollack, the saithe has a small barbule and has a straighter lateral line. It feeds over rocks and fairly near the surface, and is usually caught with a team of white feathered flies kept on the move with a bamboo rod. Its colour is olive green above and silvery white below. The pollack has a golden tinge on its belly. It feeds in deeper water than the saithe and is trolled for by spinning rubber worms or jigging a team of coloured flies vertically. The flesh of both these fish is on the soft side, so it pays to salt and dry them—of which, more later. In this form they are as good to eat as salt cod or ling. If eaten fresh, sprinkle fillets with salt and leave overnight.

Tope. Runs up to 6 feet in length and weighs up to 70 lb. In shape, it is shark-like with a blue-grey back and a white belly. Bait, as for conger, should be absolutely fresh, preferably a mackerel rigged on two large hooks. For some reason it is not a good lobster bait, but when skinned and cooked with imagination makes a tasty, bone-free meal. Very popular on the Mediterranean, also with our fried fish shops.

Ling. Reddish brown above, white below. Looks rather like a sawn-off conger with a rounded tail. Bait and habitat same as conger, and is at its best when salted and dried.

Salmon. Although a sea fish, it uses rivers to spawn. It is only landable by licensed fishermen who have to conform to many regulations. The law lays down that the unlicensed catching of salmon by line or net is illegal, and that any salmon caught must be returned to the water alive or dead. This calls for compliance (or a wary eye!).

Mackerel. Any description would be superfluous. It comes inshore early in May and remains thereabouts until October. They seldom take a baited hook but respond voraciously to all forms of small spinning gear and feathered hooks. In fact anything resembling a small fish, which is their main food. Also caught in drift and seine nets.

There are many fish other than the ones described and for purpose of identification Travers-Jenkins book on "The Fishes of the British Isles", published by Warne, is most informative.

Study the Grounds

In bottom fishing by hand, either from boat or shore, any of the fish I have described are likely to be caught, with the possible exception of salmon, mullet or mackerel. In this type of fishing it is most important to have some idea of the grounds where fish are feeding at various states of the tide. These grounds, or marks, are well known locally but there is no reason why charts should not be studied and fancy backed.

Charts have the bottom marked as follows: S, sand; ST, stones; R, rocks; M, mud; SH, shell; G, gravel. An armed lead will also help. By armed I mean a thickly greased indentation in the lead bottom to which samples will adhere.

Luck in finding a productive ground will depend on various factors, including the availability of food in the area and the state of the tide. Feed, I have found to move about the same way as the fish, all in search of a living. Most productive tide times range from one hour before slack, low, to two hours flood.

The most successful amateur I knew split his yearly holiday into three- or four-day periods when low slacks were nearest dawn and dusk. If the weather was boat-worthy he spent his tide times at sea with a couple of rods, one light and baited with worm or mussel and the other heavy baited with a lump of fish. By this method he covered all sizes that might be in the vicinity.

If conditions were unsuitable for a boat, he fly-fished a rock channel for pollack and bass, using various lures. His most successful was a scruffy-looking brown fly made by dressing the shank of a long hook with dark brown wool and feathering it with a couple of hackles from the neck of a brown hen. To me it looked like a piece of seaweed in the water but it was a sure killer.

Good Bottom Gear

His bottom gear was interesting. Instead of using wire paternosters, he rigged the business end of the line by swivelling three pieces of celluloid to a thickish piece of gut. These yards were 6 inches long and ½ inch wide, the inner ends being heated and bent over a pin slightly larger than the gut, and glued. They were attached by threading onto the gut, which was knotted off at 9-inch intervals. Glass beads were positioned between knot and yard to ensure tidal swivelling.

On the lower yard a hook was rigged on an 18-inch piece of gut and on the upper ones the gut was about 6 inches long. When boat fishing he took along with him, to attach to his anchor, a small mesh bag filled with fish offal which, according to him, gave an attractive tidal trace. Whether it worked this way or not I do not know, but feel sure it would attract small crabs away from worrying at the legitimate bait.

Before I go on to the professional side of long lining, something might be learnt from another friend of mine. Boats were not for him. He fished off the shore when he considered conditions were right. These were a cold, preferably autumn, day with enough on-shore wind to stir up the water. His gear consisted of four hand lines, a small wind dodger that he rigged on three sticks, and a folding stool. The four lines fitted with wire paternosters were set to fish about 20 yards apart. Each was attached to a 2-foot stake topped off with a salvaged umbrella rib carrying a small bell at the top.

When set, he took up position in his canvas lee and proceeded to look and listen. His weights were interesting. One was a piece of flattened lead pipe with a couple of nails driven half-way through to give added anchorage. This chilly method is fair enough for those who can take it, and I must say he got results, mostly whiting and an occasional bass.

Long lining comes under two headings, the "small" and the "great". The former runs up to 500 hooks of haddock size and the quarry is cod, haddock, whiting, flat fish, etc. It is baited with mussel or worm, laid preferably across a flood and only allowed to fish for a very few hours. If left any longer it will be found that the bigger fish, dog, tope and skate, help themselves to the catch. It can be set from a boat or along the shore at low tide. If the latter, baits should be covered with a little sand, otherwise there will be a gull or two to deal with.

Although there are places where long lining pays off handsomely, in my parish it was hopeless to line for the smaller fish due to a heavy infestation of small green crabs who pounced on the bait as soon as it bottomed.

A Fish Mystery

Queer things happen below, and one of the strangest was told me by Captain Eric Croft, senior fishery officer for the northern division of the Lancashire and Western Sea Fishery district. There are some sands near his house on Morecambe Bay where trawling is absolutely useless, yet they are outstandingly good when fished with lines, sometimes rigged with pins instead of hooks. Don't laugh—our ancestors success-fully used thorns for fishing (see Fig. 14). Captain Croft tried to solve the mystery by setting a line and then arranging with the Fishery patrol boat to trawl along both sides. Result, not a fin in the trawl, but when the line was recovered it carried an average catch. I mention this fact to demonstrate the fishes' mysterious way of life.

The "great" line is similar in make-up to the "small" but with larger hooks and considerably stronger lines. It is usually laid by the deep-sea "liners" literally by the mile, their quarry being halibut, hake, turbot, conger, large dogs, tope and skate. For bait, pieces of herring, mackerel or squid are used.

Fig. 14.   The forerunner of hooks. "The set line will often beat the trawl."

During early spring Huw and I worked shortish lengths, about 100 hooks each, of "great" line in order to help ourselves to the incoming—for spawning—skate or ray which, when winged, found a ready market both locally and inland. Bait used was herring which, of course, we had to buy.

One Workable Way

There are several ways of readying long lines but we found the most workable was, when baiting, to coil the main line down into a basket and stick or hang baited hooks around the side. Large swivel hooks were used for the simple reason that they could be detached through the swivel if the line got into a snarl which it usually did on recovery. Fish were removed from the line as they came aboard by a disgorger made up of a $\frac{3}{8}$-inch steel rod with a V cut in the end. In addition to skate we caught many unsaleable dogs. These were split, salted and dried for future use as pot bait.

For the smaller fish, taken on hand or "small" line, I found that the most attractive bait was undoubtedly the mussel. I, too, agree with the fish—it is my favourite sea food. Shelling is a knack and calls for a good deal of practice, so don't be discouraged if quite a few meats get mangled in the process. The mussel should be pressed tightly on the forefinger by the thumb, and inserting a special double-edged or pointed knife at the point marked X, slide it around, thereby cutting through the topmost membrane attachment (see Fig. 15). Prise the shell open and break off at hinge. If, I repeat if, the operation

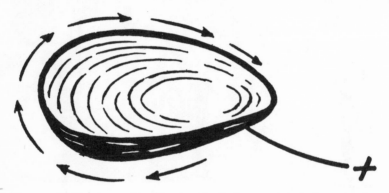

FIG. 15. Shelling a mussel is a knack and calls for a good deal of practice. See directions in text.

has been carried out correctly, the meat will be lying in the bottom shell, and is removed by running the knife around and cutting through the remaining shell attachment. It is baited by sticking the hook through the hinge end and, with a couple of twists, burying it in the flesh.

If mussels are not readily available, lug worms can be used with similar results. They are to be found between high and low tide and can be spotted by their curly sand casts. Do not dig at random amongst the casts unless you use a strong garden fork, otherwise you will find that your catch will mostly consist of spade-cut corpses.

Professional worm diggers use the following method. About 9 inches away from the cast will be seen a dimple in the sand. If there are, which is most likely, a conglomeration of casts, the spade is inserted for a couple of inches into a dimple and rocked to and fro. A water bubbling will be seen at one of the casts, which means that the worm is lying head towards the dimple in a U-shaped tunnel. A good spadeful is taken out of the dimple end, then the spade is worked back towards the cast with a scraping motion, and with luck there will be an undamaged bait. The sand-filled end of the sea worm is useless, and should be pinched off and discarded.

In times of dire shortage I have used, with varying success, large earth worms. Baiting is similar to the mussel, hook goes through the head, and again with a couple of twists through the body.

In this chapter I have given the basic facts about the baited line. These could be applied practically throughout the world but as conditions vary so much it is up to the reader to work out the most suitable for his own district. Bait, of course, is subject to availability.

Chapter 12

Some Successful Lures
and their use

THE great advantage of artificial lures is that they dispense with the work of obtaining bait and loading the baited line. The lures represent, as far as is known, immature fish food and must be kept on the move through the water by trolling, or jigging, which consists of an up and down movement of the arm, while drifting or at anchor. For successful working, one must have a fairly accurate knowledge of feeding areas and best states of tides. Really sharp, clean hooks are essential, the brightness of the hook having a lot to do with success.

The most productive tool of the trade is known as a rag line (see Fig. 16) though feathered serpent would be more descriptive of make-up, and at times its vile behaviour. It consists of a length of gut weighted at one end and a dozen or more flies on their separate gut droppers.

The tyro is advised to start the exercise with half that number of flies, as a dozen mackerel, or worse still, pollack, going haywire alongside the boat take some handling and hook dodging.

There are two ways of handling the catch, the first being to allow them to gyrate alongside and unhooking them singly as they come aboard.

The other, which in my opinion is both easier and safer, is to haul in the complete catch and dump them together with lead weight into two boxes placed end to end. Starting from the after box mackerel can be cleared single-handed by grasping the hook shank with finger and thumb, swinging over in a half circle and fetching the fish up with a bump against the inner edge of the box. It will be found that the hook tears clear.

Pollack being larger, and with bigger mouths, call for

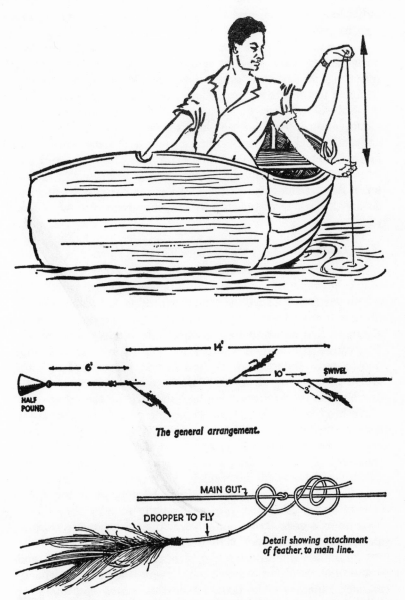

The general arrangement.

FIG. 16.   Rag line or feathered serpent, showing detail of setting and operation.
Motor Boat & Yachting.

individual attention, and a disgorger is useful. It saves tooth-torn fingers.

If you wish to make your own serpents the following gear must be obtained: 15-foot lengths of heavy pollack gut; a coil of lighter mackerel gut to make the droppers which, when attached to the vertical gut, should be 3 or 4 inches in length; a supply of haddock hooks; a reel of silk for whipping; some blood-coloured nail varnish; longish, flexible feathers from the nape of a cockerel's neck, some brown and some white. The natural coloured feathers can be used as they are, and the white dyed to any fancied colour. The reason for this is that when fish are sluggish or thin on the patch they are inclined to go for the colour of the day. It may be green, yellow, red or white.

How to Start

Start operations by whipping gut and feather to the hook shank, finishing up with a few half-hitches topped off with a blob of nail varnish. This will secure the whipping and give the lure a bloodshot eye. Soak all gut in water until reasonably pliable, although nylon or perlon twines are mostly used today. The main gut is then knotted at 1-foot intervals and loops tied in both ends for weight and line attachment. The knots are to position the droppers which are attached by a double overhand knot on one side and a half-hitch on the other.

All hitches must be on the same side of the gut positioning knot as the flies must lie "towards up" when in action. Two conical weights, one about 2 lb. and the other 8 oz. will be required. To rig the line, attach lower loop in the main gut to half a fathom of line which will carry the weight. The length of the upper or handling line will depend on the depth fished. Some fishermen prefer a weight heavier than 8 oz. because in a good strike, some fish will swim over one another and a real "cats cradle" is the result.

Commence operations by attaching the 2-lb. weight and tow around at about 3 m.p.h. until there is a sizeable strike of mackerel then stop the boat, attach the lighter lead and start jigging the line up and down.

Pollack grounds are usually found around and amongst weedy rocks, their feeding places seeming to change with the direction of tidal stream, usually to leeward. I think the best way to find their grounds is to tow a rubber worm on a single line until there is a strike or two in the same area. When found, drop the feather line and try to remain in the same place, even if it means anchoring.

When going into action with this professional weapon you will, in all probability, land a sizeable catch and wonder what the deuce to do with it. Remember the local fishermen, due to the usual shortage of ice, have to rely on selling in the locality and if you give fish away, you are knocking the bottom out of their slender market. They would prefer you, if you are

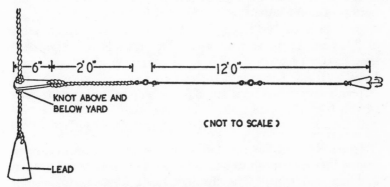

Fig. 17.   Mackerel line and spinner. "Mackerel feed at all heights, so it pays to have some heavy weights."

so minded, to sell them at ruling prices or better still let them have them for disposal or salting down for pot-bait, thereby retaining their regard and, who knows, their help in other directions.

The most sporting and productive way of fishing for mackerel is by the traditional trolling method. Four lines can be fished from the same boat if the two forward carry heavier weights and are fished with a fathom or so shorter lines than the after ones. The rig from the lead to the spinner is most important and should carry several swivels (see Fig. 17). Mackerel feed at all heights, and contrary to belief, spend a lot of their time near the bottom. For this reason it pays to have some very heavy leads, say up to 4 lb., the normal being about 2 lb. I have found that the most suitable are conical in shape with rounded bottoms. To facilitate weight changing a quick release tackle snap may be used.

Many Different Lures

There are a multiplicity of lures used by fishermen and most of them rely on brightness of hook for attraction, which can be increased by scraping or polishing the lead sinker. The quarry is mostly cod and haddock but as neither fish abound in my sea parish, results, apart from whiting and codling, were negligible. This, of course, may not apply to other districts so do not be put off by my experience. Lures are jigged at feeding height which for this type of fishing is usually very near the bottom. Good results can be obtained if the lower arms of the serpent, or hooks on the jig, are armed with small bright pieces of fish skin. As the serpent and other jigs rely on brightness, they should be washed off in fresh water and dried after use. Even with this treatment, springiness seems to go out of the serpent's droppers after a few days' fishing so it pays to re-arm it with both droppers and flies. Some other types of lures are described below. Names vary according to locality.

Sprule. Rectangular piece of lead 4 inches in length tapering from ¾ inch at bottom to ⅜ inch at top. Drill holes near bottom and top and thread line through, back knotting to keep it static. Whip on largish hooks about 1½ inches from lead, which should be brightened before fishing (see Fig. 18).

Murderer. Flattish and fish-like in form with two sizeable cod hooks cast in when moulding. Scrape lead bright before jigging (see Fig. 18).

Dandy. Works well on herring and whiting if they are present in quantity. Four or more pieces of ⅛-inch wire are hitched centrally, at 8-inch intervals, to the line, then pieces of gut, armed with haddock hooks, are attached with thread along the brass wires as shown in diagram. A touch of nail varnish will keep hitches and whipping from slipping. No bait is necessary but hooks must be very bright. The answer would be chromium plated or stainless hooks on all lures if these were obtainable (see Fig. 18).

Rubber Eels. These can be bought in many colours. Red is

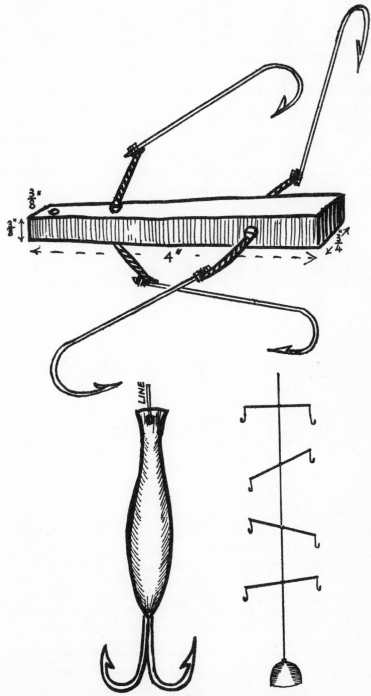

FIG. 18. The sprule, murderer, (or jigger) and dandy.

the most attractive, but if this fails, try white, green, silver or brown. Choosy things, pollack.

This short list does not by any means exhaust the many different sorts of lures in use, but is merely intended to give the basic principles.

Chapter 13

Many Ways of Catching Fish

BEFORE getting down to the onshore or near shore side of net fishing, it might be as well to take a look at what is known of the methods employed since prehistoric times, as this type of fishing has altered little in application since those days. The following historical guesses are extracts from a Ministry publication "Fishing gear of England and Wales", written many years ago by Mr. Davies, a Ministry scientist. An even greater elaboration of methods is now given in a fascinating book by Dr. A. von Brandt entitled "Fish Catching Methods of the World" issued by Fishing News (Books) Ltd.

Obviously man progressed with the quantity capture of sea-fish very early in his existence. This has been proved by excavations into the shell mounds. One on Oransay indicated that Neolithic man fed on tope, dogfish, wrasse, skate and edible crabs, including the fiddler. During this period, about 10,000 years ago, the seas and rivers were teeming with fish which could easily be caught with the most primitive gear. Precisely how they were caught is unknown but as they were taken in quantity it is likely that there was some form of trap or weir built of stones or wattles. This of course could quite easily be made by walling the mouths of sea-going streams or estuary gutters, and would leave the catch high and dry at low water.

Alternatively, a stone-and-wattle barrier might be constructed across the channel between a small island and the shore. The fish could pass round the outside of the island, then shorewards on the flood, but would be held by the barrier when attempting to make their way seawards on the ebb. An example of this method is to be found near Menai Bridge in Anglesey. This system of fishing is dependent on the existence of a tidal channel; an open shore would require a modified type of barrier—V-shaped, with its apex pointing in the direction of the ebb tide. Fish making inshore on the flood could easily pass this obstruction, but on their return with the ebb would be stranded at the apex.

The introduction, at some unknown date, of the baited hook line marked an immense step forward in the technique of fishing. The hook, as we know it, was developed from a thorn or a tiny stick sharpened at both ends; when swallowed it would stick across the throat and hold secure. This method is still in use around our coasts for the capture of flatfish, and is known as the pin line.

Nets and Netting

Next came the art of net making, which must have originated in the Mediterranean, as the fishermen there had no tides to help them. They had, therefore, to devise a means of enclosing the fish and dragging them towards the shore, thereby evolving the seine net as known to-day. Some indication of its origin comes from its name, which in classical Greek is sagene; conceivably it may have christened the French river Seine on its way north.

The art of net-making undoubtedly reached this country with the Mediterranean tribes who spread along the western littoral of Europe many thousands of years B.C. In all probability it emanated from Egypt, where pictures have been found in tombs showing fishermen working an enclosing net, or seine. The Egyptians made good ropes of papyrus and other fibres at least 5,000 years ago, and as they were notable fish-eaters, they doubtless contrived an efficient form of net. Nets would also be used for the capture of water fowl which, with the fish, were salted, sun-dried, and sent to inland markets.

The netting knot, known as the sheet bend, has remained the same through the ages, as is proved by the fragments of net, identical with modern ones, which have been found in excavations of Swiss lake villages. Until quite recently twines were spun from plant fibres, though to-day these are rapidly being replaced by man-made synthetics which give increased breaking strain and resistance to rot. The synthetics industry is, indeed, proving of immense value to commercial fishermen. Not only does it provide long-lasting and considerably lighter gear, but also their protective clothing, which is now based on p.v.c., and which has entirely ousted the heavy, sticky oilskin of the past hundred years or so. Corks and floats, too, are obsolescent, their place rapidly being taken by a synthetically expanded material which shows about a two-to-one floatation advantage on cork, is practically impervious to water intake, and resists abrasion.

Meanwhile, the coming of the net gave the fisherman greater mobility, on both shore and river pitches. Moreover, by weighting the bottom and floating the top he could drag the net towards the shore, safely enclosing any fish when the two ends were landed. At this period the fishing boat appeared, and it was no longer necessary for man to be shorebound in his fishing. In its earliest phase the boat consisted merely of bundles of reeds lashed together into a raft-like structure. This was followed by a dug-out canoe, the skin-covered coracle, and eventually by the overlapping plank or "clinker" construction familiar to-day. Henceforward it is easy to visualise the boat-drawn trawl, which, after all, is only some form of open-mouthed bag, drawn through the water at varying depths. Possibly the net was kept open by being dragged along between two boats, in a fashion still used by the coracle fishermen of Wales.

Early Trawls

As early as 1376 there are records of a trawl net known as the Wondychoun, from which the modern beam trawl has been evolved. Apparently this was the start of the immature-fish-killing controversy, which is still active to-day. In a petition for its prohibition in the reign of Edward III, it was complained "that this craftily made net, in the form of an oyster dredge, presses so hard on the bottom that it destroys all life". Most of the early information on fishing methods comes from the time of the early Stuarts, when there were numerous prosecutions for the suppression of bottom-trawling in order to preserve the fisheries, but opposition diminished slightly in the year 1616, when the king's fishmonger was granted a dispensation "to trawl for plaice and soles in such places as he can best find them".

The next development took place in the late 19th century, when the modern otter trawl came into use. This dispensed with the cumbersome beam and the difficulty of deck stowage. It was easier on man-power and, owing to its increased spread, allowed greater areas of bottom to be searched.

Having looked at the past, what of the present and of the future? There are other interesting developments. One of them is the catching in the Caspian Sea of an anchovy-like fish known as the kilka. This is done by a submerged electric light working in conjunction with a suction hose lowered to the correct depth. Fish attracted by the light are sucked in and pumped to the fish hold where the water is drawn off.

Remarkable progress has been made in electrical fishing, from the stunning and collection of predatory fish such as pike, in the inland waters, to the attraction of fish towards nets and fish pumps in the open sea. With trawls, electricity can be used to a double advantage. It improves the condition of the catch by reducing the period of death struggle, while electrodes are employed to attract fish to the mouth of the trawl. Fish caught in normal trawls are gathered in the congested space of the cod end, where struggling causes the muscles to produce a considerably higher degree of fatigue, which affects the quality of the flesh. Electrocution hastens the progress of rigor mortis, and thereby facilitates the ultimate processing.

Future Possibilities

It is conceivable that in the future fish will be dehydrated immediately when caught, by a process similar to that used in the production of blood plasma. Experiments along these lines are being carried out and the resultant product, feather-light and vacuum-packed will, when soaked in the correct volume of water, return to its pristine sea freshness. With world population growing at its present rate, the time will undoubtedly come when we shall have to harvest the oceans in real earnest. So far our knowledge of these waters is limited, but we are rapidly learning more of the biological aspect. The basic sea food is plankton, which sustains the bulk of all marine life, and it may well have to be pressed into mankind's service. This high-protein food, suitably processed, may form an important part of the diet of coming generations.

With future fish shortages in mind, the French are experimenting with the idea of a fish farmhouse on the sea bed inhabited by skin-diving farmers. One is inclined to keep an open mind on the usefulness of this trial, but extraordinary things do come to pass. Skin diving is already paying off dividends in the collection of scientific knowledge about the private lives of fish, and the behaviour of fishing gear in action. British scientists are doing excellent work on the conservation of fish stocks. To me, the most interesting side of their work—and I am sure it has an immense future—is the rearing or farming of immatures from the egg until they reach a size sufficient to enable them to avoid many of the predators. So far, this scheme is limited to the production of flatfish, lobsters and salmon. To be successful this will have to be handled on an international scale, coupled with an agreement on mesh sizes.

I am told that in Norway they have gone a step further, and are actually breeding salmon in captivity up to marketable size. A wonderful achievement, as we know that salmon spend most of their lives at sea, only using rivers for spawning and immature growth. If this is a financial success it will certainly spread to this country and make up in some way for the losses sustained by the salmon family caused by the criminal pollution, by man, of so many of our rivers.

Chapter 14

Inshore Netting Gives
Good Results

NOWADAYS shore netting only seems to be taken seriously
on very few parts of our coastline. In my opinion it should
be re-developed as there are so many places, mostly estuarial,
where it could add extra income to the part-time fisherman.
The operational word is "part" as inshore fishing must, due to
its seasonal nature, be backed by another source of income. My
introduction to this type of fishing was when I was sent by
"Fishing News" up to the Morecambe Bay area to inquire into
the depredations on the cockle beds by that attractive little bird,
the Oyster Catcher. Its numbers had increased, since protection came in, at such an alarming rate that it was being blamed
(and quite rightly so) for the rundown to near-nil of the cockle
population in the area. Two years before, the annual catch, or
rather pick, from Flookborough sands amounted, so I was
told, to £24,000.

By the time I got up there the pick was down to almost nil
and Ministry scientists had completed a survey and found an
astronomic increase in the number of oyster catchers. A number
were shot for stomach examination and it was found that in
every case the intestinal tract was full of immature cockle
remains. The birds were removed from the protection list and
ways discussed for their reduction.

Arrangements were made for the erection of fly nets, sited
at the edge of high water mark. The reason for this was to
ensure that other types caught in the mesh would not drown
and could be released. This worked very well for a time,
oyster catchers were destroyed, other types being boxed and
sent off for ringing and release.

But (there usually is a "but" in these things) the bird-loving fraternity threatened legal action if this method was continued. The threat floored the exercise, so rocket nets were tried. Again the bird lovers stepped in: "you can only use rocket nets for ringing even if birds are off the protection list". Advice was again taken by the Ministry who were in charge of the job, and someone came up with the idea that the operative word was "rocket". It was thought that the law could be circumvented if the guide sticks carrying the net were discharged from guns. It was tried, but without much success, as the feeding grounds were immense and difficult to work.

So it was abandoned in favour of gunfire in order to harass and if possible move on the flocks. Whether it worked this way or not I cannot say, but shortly afterwards there was a large build-up of oyster catchers on the cockle beds of South Wales. Possibly the pickings were better.

Man of Many Parts

While I was at Morecambe I met Mr Billy Burrow, a man of many parts: salmon fisherman, sand guide (low water mark was seven miles away in places) and before the Bird Protection Act put him out of business, a gunner and fly netter. His catch, he told me, was bagged and railed off to London twice a week. All was grist to the mill. Mallard fetched sixpence each, oyster catchers twopence and the smaller fry, such as stint, turnstones, ring plover, etc. a penny apiece. According to him the smaller fry doubled for snipe on the table of the unsuspecting London gourmets, and it is hoped they also found their way into that famous Fleet Street lark, steak and oyster pudding in lieu of one of our most attractive songsters.

Sand guiding in the old days was an important job as, before reasonable roads were built, both foot and wheeled traffic could avoid many weary miles by crossing the River Kent Estuary at low water. To-day it is limited to bevvies of tourists who have a mind to cross just for the hell of it but they must still move in convoy.

I spent a very amusing evening with Billy (Plate VII p. 68) at Guide Farm and the tape taken on my portable recorder of his garrulous yarns is amongst my most treasured possessions. These, delivered in the broadest of dialect, told of fish, wild fowl and a river board bailiff, with the accent on the latter.

Apparently towards the end of the season he got into a battle royal with a young and inexperienced bailiff who found that the mesh on Billy's salmon haaf net did not meet with his approval. Billy, when charged, with tongue in cheek, feigned remorse and did not object to the confiscation of his net but was not at all surprised when he found the net quietly replaced in his yard the following day.

The joke which lost nothing in the telling recoiled on the embryo bailiff as the law lays down a minimum size of mesh. Billy's net happened to be in excess of the limit, but as it did not fit the measuring gauge, the bailiff thought he had a sitter. Billy also used the legal hand net or "butterfly" for chasing salmon about the shallows. To operate it successfully one must have the eyes of a hawk and the legs of a hare. Billy had both, and had in fact been using them for upwards of seventy years.

Story of a Gun

In the rafters I noticed the stockless remains of an 8-bore gun, and asked about it. Billy told me that like most wild-fowlers he had his own ideas on the powder charge and size of shot to penetrate the feathered breastplate of an oncoming goose. He came to the conclusion that the propellent charge should be increased and that lead pellets for shot were too soft; so he got hold of some rock blasting black powder and robbed an old bicycle of its ball bearings. The resultant self-loaded cartridge went into the breach and himself into a sand scrape on the evening flight line.

Conditions were perfect. In came a skein of geese flying low. He drew a bead ahead of the leader—and passed out amongst the resultant roar of discharge! When he came to, it was dark and he staggered homewards. The following day he found the gun barrels but as far as he knew the stock was space-borne sputnik-wise!

I tried to get him to tell me the ways of shore stake netting, but his interests lay in the defeat of salmon and wild-fowl. He did, however, take me the following day to see his brother Ike who made a seasonal living with stake nets. The upshot was that Ike took me under his wing and asked me to report for duty well before dawn the following morning, which turned out to be as black and as wet as the inside of a windless cow.

Mr D. G. Harrison, Fishery Officer for the district, turned
up to give Ike a hand with his nets having heard that he
wasn't too fit—typical of this grand man, an ex-fisherman who,
in spite of his many similar kindnesses, ruled his district with a
rod of iron. Sea fishing laws, aimed at conservation, are very
sensible, being framed in the interests of fishermen.

From Shrimps to Salmon

Mr Harrison, who was due for a tour of his district which
stretched from Arnside to the Cumberland border, kindly

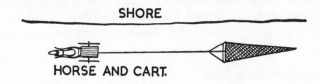

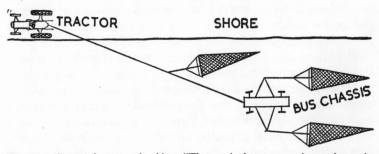

FIG. 19. Cart and tractor shanking. "The net is drawn over the sands on the
incoming tide. Average catch (depending on season) 6 gallons of shrimp."

took me along and introduced me to other inshoremen who,
due to his friendly influence, bent over backwards to show me
their diverse methods of shore netting, their quarry ranging
from shrimps to salmon. Our first call was Flookborough
where sand netting of all varieties is practised. It is famous for
the quality of its wares both from the sea and market garden.
There are many outward signs of success in the village which
are the fruits of immensely hard labour by the community.

They work every weekday tide, which ebbs away into the
far distance, tend their market gardens, shell shrimps, and for

good measure hawk their wares by means of fast-looking vans to retail customers living far inland.

Here I met Mr Billy Butler, whose establishment fits neatly into the above pattern. He had just arrived off the sands after an early morning's cart shanking (see Plate VII) and his catch, about 6 gallons, was average for the time of year. He told me that with the coming of sustained frosts shrimps would go deep and shanking would end until about March.

The following morning I was out on the sands where I saw some twenty carts working. In addition, there were three tractors working double nets. Due to the high cost of maintenance and frequent bogging down, this new idea is not making much headway, so it is likely that horse traction will remain paramount.

Fishing With a Cart

It must also be remembered that the stake netsman uses a cart in lieu of a boat. His horse is kept in the finest fettle and well he might be as, apart from the friendly company he gives out on the sandy wastes, he is the only form of life-insurance if one is being beaten by the fast-flowing flood.

Flookborough, as far as I know, is the only place to have a lighthouse, or rather an occulting light high up on a pole to guide fishermen off the sands. Low springs really are up to seven miles seaward in places, and the flood tide runs in faster than a man can run. If the weather turns misty, navigation can be a very dodgy business. Happily, horses have some sense of direction which is checkable with a pocket compass; also the horses are great swimmers. I should hate to be caught out on the sands with a tractor outfit. Ike Burrow of Kents Bank told me that in thick weather he carries a bundle of leafy twigs, sticking one into the sand every 20 yards or so on his walk to the nets from where he leaves his boat in the channel.

As previously arranged we embarked with Ike Burrow and joined the sea-going ebb in the channel which rapidly swilled us down to the stream nets (see Fig. 20) about a couple of miles out on the sands. These were set parallel to the sand ripple line on a bank formed by a slight curve in the channel. There were three nets, in length about 40 yards, spaced about 50 yards apart.

When we arrived, the shore ends of the nets were drying out and fish could be seen lying in the hammock-like pocket formed by the fast-flowing ebb. Mr Harrison cleared the nets, then proceeded to check stakes for stability, and any found loose were tightened by a few blows from an apple-wood mallet.

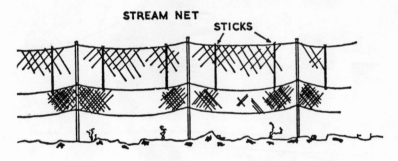

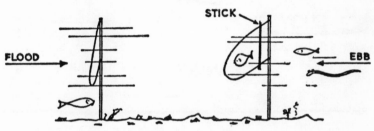

FIG. 20.   The Stream net.

Using a Stream Net

The stream net, so named because it can only be fished in fast-running water, is secured to stakes driven in at 9-foot intervals to which both head and footrope are attached. These are kept apart by short intervening sticks that hold the net open against the strong tide. The footrope is set about 10 inches off the ground, to allow fish to pass underneath on the flood. It surprised me that the net fished at all, but I was told that the run forced the fish off the bottom during the ebb, when they were on their way to lie up in deeper water.

Having completed these tasks, we towed the boat up-channel, which had practically dried out, and rejoined Mr Burrow,

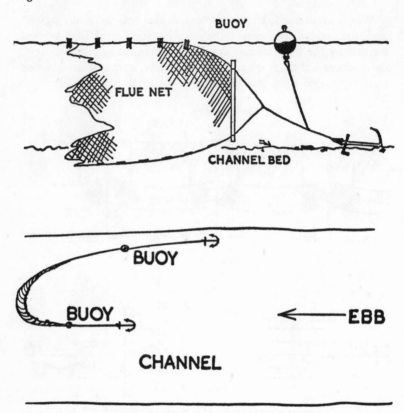

BUOY

FLUE NET

CHANNEL BED

BUOY

BUOY

←——— EBB

CHANNEL

POSSER

FIG. 21. Flue net and posser. "The posser is plunged downwards into the water and the explosion-like plop scares fish off the bottom and into the net."

whom we had dropped earlier about a mile up-channel to explore a new bank that was forming. He would know if flatfish were feeding there, by docks or fish-shaped depressions in the sand, also by tiny piles of excreted shells. Our catch of about 50 lb. of flatties was sufficient to satisfy that day's customer requirements.

Then I was taken upstream for a demonstration of the flue net. Lengths and depths of this vary according to the ground being worked. This particular net was about 60 yards long and 12 feet in depth. The headrope is corked and the footrope fairly heavily leaded.

First an anchor is dropped upstream and the net paid out in the form of a letter J and another anchor dropped. By this time the net, due to current action, will have formed itself into a sort of ramp, the bottom of which will be lying on the ground. The boat is then backed off and rowed up toward the concave face, coming gradually nearer while a disturbance is created by means of an extraordinary looking tool known as a "posser" (see Fig. 21). This is simply made by attaching a metal cone to the end of a longish pole. It is plunged, cone downwards, into the water and the resultant explosive plop scares fish off the bottom and into the net. The net is recovered from the downstream end by bringing corks and leads together, thus forming a fish-enclosing bag. Two drags produced about 40 lb. of flatties of various varieties, but as these were surplus to requirements they were returned to the water.

With the assistance of Mr Harrison, I was able to get down to the business of describing various other nets I had seen, and I hope that the descriptions and sketches I have been able to produce will enable readers to grasp the general principles involved.

Stake Nets

Since stake nets in general form a permanent barrier and hinder the passage of fish to the feeding grounds, some method has to be employed to give free access on the flood and closure on the ebb. The best example of this is the Balk net used in the Morecambe Bay area, and the description of one used there will serve the general purpose.

The set, which is in crescent form, must not exceed 300 yards, and consists of up to fifteen nets, set by the third to 20 yards, fourteen meshes deep of $1\frac{3}{4}$-inch bar. The headline, set on stakes about 18 inches above ground, is therefore deeper than the actual height of the net, thus allowing a certain amount of bagginess. The footrope is only attached to the ten or eleven outer stakes at each end and every sixth stake between.

In between stakes to which the footrope is not attached, there is an arrangement known as the "Balk" or riding stake.

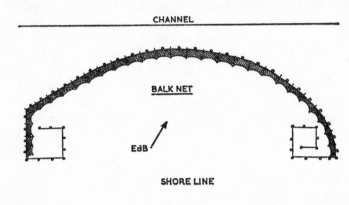

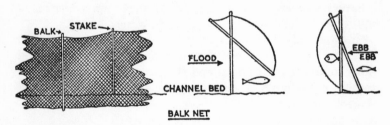

FIG. 22.   Balk net on riding stake. This net operates simply with the rise and fall of the tide.

This is simply a loose stake of about 2 inches diameter at one end tapering down to 1 inch at the other, with a length of 4 feet. The thick end is attached to the footrope with a half-hitch and a twist, and the other to the headrope in a like manner (see Fig. 22).

Now it is obvious that, when the flood strikes the net, it will lift the lower end of the balk and allow fish to pass through to the feeding grounds. When the tide turns the opposite will ensue, the butt ends of the balk being forced against the ground, causing the net to become a barrier. A similar, but shorter and more portable net is known as the "tail". It works more or less on the same principle, but has a tail or cod end attached. Both the tail net and bag net have a form of non-return valve to hold the catch.

The only sand net I saw not worked on this trapping principle was the "stream" which I have previously dealt with. This, of course, can only be used where there is a very strong flow of water over the banks.

"Haaf" Net

Salmon fishing being out of season, I was unable to see the famous "Haaf" at work on the channels, so I will settle for a

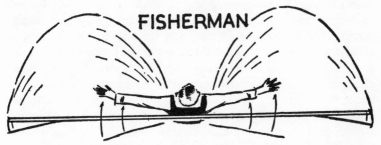

FIG. 23.   Salmon Haaf net. Very successful in the hands of an expert.

short description (see Fig. 23). It has a beam of 16 feet, a middle stick of 6 feet, and side sticks of 4 feet 6 inches. The net is made by chaining out fifty-four meshes of 2-inch bar and braiding to a depth of 21 feet. Twenty-two meshes are laid out after doubling over and half meshing the selvages on each side stick, and the rest are distributed along top and bottom of the net.

The method of working is for the fisherman to stand in the tide at the river or channel edge holding the middle stick over his shoulder with the bag streaming out behind him. As soon as a fish is felt to strike the net, the bag is thrown over the beam, thus enclosing it. I must admit I am rather hazy on this latter point as I did not see the net in action.

Our most northerly call was at Barrow, where I met Mr Nicholas, who works a variety of nets in the Duddon Estuary, including trammels, which I will deal with later. A very interesting piece of information I picked up from Mr Nicholas was that he uses his "posser" to drive fish into trammels set in water up to 30 feet in depth.

A Useful Home made Net

One net I did not see in action on the Lancashire sands is, in my opinion, the most simple and useful of tools, whether fishing for the household pot, lobster bait, or local market, and can be used on almost any shore. I first saw it used by quite an aged lady who made the major portion of her income by winkle gathering. Her net was a very home-made affair and consisted of an old rabbit long-net, originally 100 yards long, cut in two and doubled to give extra height—it fished about 4 feet high. The headline was corked along the top and a few stones hitched to the footrope to give sinkage. Her catch usually consisted of bass and sea-trout. Any fish too big to get trapped by the mesh seemed to get the fine thread tangled in its teeth and held fast, and even smaller fish which would have slipped through the mesh sometimes got tooth-tangled. I think her success was greatly due to the bagginess of the net. The net was given bagginess by setting it to the head and footropes by the half, and by the half I mean that if a sheet of netting was stretched out straight and measured 100 yards the finished net would measure 50 yards when set to the ropes. Normally, nets of this type are set on by the third (100 yards stretched, 66 yards when roped) but I found that for beach setting they were far more inclined to entangle fish if set in by about the half. The old lady's net, about 30 yards long, was held in position by a large stone tied to each end. It was set directly from high tide mark seawards, and the reason for setting one end on this mark is that fish on the feed come right inshore during the hours of darkness. The net is laid on the uncovered sand and I have found that it pays to set the last few yards of the seaward end back into a sort of tick-shaped trap, held in place by two ropes attached to stones which are judicously placed.

Stones being difficult to attach, I cast, in concrete, a few flattish cheese-shaped weights of about 40 lb. each with an incast ring for attachment. Originally I used anchors, but found this to be a mistake as the shore anchor tended to drag seawards through the soft sand. This allowed the outer end of the net to snag and lift the outer anchor, causing the gear to become tide-borne towards an unknown destination.

My shore nets had a depth of 7 feet and were 60 yards long (100 yards stretched) with a courlene headline of 1½-inch circumference, carrying 3½-inch diameter plastic floats placed at 4-foot intervals. Size for size, plastic floats have about 40 per cent more buoyancy than corks and as corks are irregular-surfaced they incline to snag on the finer man-made fibres of 2-inch knot to knot mesh which can be of nylon, terylene or ulstron. As synthetic fibres are considerably stronger, size for size, than the vegetable variety, a finer and more effective size can be used. One important point is that the meshes should be double knotted, otherwise they will most surely slip. Ordinary leads along a footrope can be a damnable nuisance on this type of net as they are inclined to fall through and tangle with the meshes while the net is thrashing around in an onshore breeze. A recent innovation that does away with this trouble is a smooth synthetic footrope (now readily obtainable) fitted with a lead core.

Advice on Seals

Grey seals were a worrying factor during the herring and salmon season. By helping themselves to the meshed fish they caused severe damage to the nets, which entailed hours of making and mending. Twm, who loved animals more than his fellow men, would take no action; his dictum being that there were plenty of fish for everyone, seals included.

Other fishermen took a different view, and asked the authorities to reduce the numbers. This took the form of a semi-official shoot which started when I was away for a few days, so I was not surprised to get a letter from Twm saying, "Come at once to stop the lords and captains of the Army who cannot shoot straight and are after hurting the poor fellows. Our Toby has been hurted."

Toby was a tame seal that Twm rescued as a tiny pup, when it was washed ashore with a damaged flipper. He housed and bottle-fed it in a waterlogged boat until it could fend for itself and follow him to sea.

I lost no time in returning and telling the gunners that we

had no objection to some seals being killed outright, but took the poorest view of snapshooting which could only end in wounding and misery. They saw the point and packed up.

As the years went by, the seal population built up to unbearable numbers and some real action had to be taken, preferably at local level where we could control things. Shooting from a moving boat into a heaving sea was out, but we did notice that both seals and our seagoing dog Topsy, a Jack Russel terrier, took an inquisitive interest in each other.

To test out an idea I had that it might be possible to bring seals into short range, Topsy and I were landed on a half tide rock where I camouflaged myself with seaweed and settled down to watch, while Topsy unhappily investigated her limited living space. After a spell, several seals surfaced and were obviously interested in Topsy, but kept their distance which was well out of certain killing range, so I quietly called Topsy in and encouraged her to howl.

The result was electric. In came the seals to investigate, right up to the edge of the rock, and the method of getting them into safe killing range was solved.

The ballistic side was settled by sending for some 12-bore cartridges, loaded with explosive balls. By explosive I mean a segmented ball covered by a thin skin of lead that makes a small hole on entrance and one the size of a basin on exit, so any impact caused instantaneous death. Fortunately it was not necessary to kill many seals, as this bloody business scared off the rest of the herd who pushed off for pastures new.

Estimates of Damage

To many, this severe action may seem to be unnecessary, but consider these facts. In the 1920s the grey seal population was estimated at 5,000 but in 1964 it was well upwards of 20,000. Dr Rae of the Torry research station, in a fairly recent report has this to say: "On conservative assumption that the present population of grey and brown seals is 20,000 and 18,000 and the assumption that the daily fish diet is 15 lb. and 11 lb. respectively, it will be seen that the loss to our dwindling inshore fisheries amounts to 220 tons daily or 80,000 tons a year."

Dr Rae also estimates that the quantity of fish consumed by seals in Scottish waters amounts to 25 per cent of the Home Water catch. In addition to the above, seals kill and discard many fish, just for the hell of it.

Should this book generate ideas of fishing for profit, even as a part-timer, the authorities governing the trade will bend over backwards to help. First comes the Ministry of Agriculture and Fisheries whose fishery enthusiasts are doing a first-class job on research, both in conservation of stocks and fishing methods. These efforts are most usefully reported on in their many publications.

The Ministry can Help

Whereas the Ministry concern themselves with all types of sea fishing, the Sea Fishery Committees that operate along our coastline are responsible solely for the control and well-being of inshore fishermen. The Committee, of which I am a member, covers the inshore coastal waters between Cumberland and Cardiganshire. In addition to a number of shore-based Fishery Officers who keep a friendly eye on matters, and run a "can I help you" service for inshoremen, the Committee owns a couple of patrol boats whose job it is to keep the bigger boats and foreigners seawards of the limit. This Committee has recently taken a look at the heavy pollution in its area and is now well forward in the process of control and abatement. This is being achieved by the appointment of a fully qualified pollution officer with a sea-going background. He is backed up by the latest developments in laboratory equipment. The Committee is made up of a cross-section of practical fishermen and representatives from contributing authorities, who are responsible for the financial side.

I am indeed fortunate in my membership of this happy ship, which is administered by Commander N. V. Craven who runs the company with a very bendable rod of iron. Fortunately our Chairman, Mr A. A. Stopford, is of the un-chairborne type; he spends most of his retired ex-banking time with the coastal fishermen, with whom he is on Christian name terms.

Not authorities, but of inestimable use to inshoremen, are Fisherman's Associations. These range from really big businesses, owning their own retail fish shops and processing plants, to the smaller ones like my local Association. Everything depends on the secretary and we are indeed fortunate in having Mr Gwilym Evans, by profession a schoolmaster, but by inclination a dyed-in-the-wool fisherman. The advantages of belonging to such an Association are many, including purchase of gear at near wholesale prices and an undertaking to assist one another in case of trouble, in other words a type of mutual salvage association. Membership is not strictly limited to professional fishermen or part-timers; boat owners of all types are welcome in an honorary capacity. The subscription, one guinea, covers membership for life. At Christmas time our secretary lays on a supper and invites members of other adjoining Associations in order that friendly and useful contacts may be maintained.

Future Prospects are Good

We are now in line with other countries with regard to inshore fishing limits. Under the West European Fisheries Convention, the limits around our shores have been extended to twelve miles, although countries that traditionally fished the three to six-mile zone were allowed to continue in that area until December, 1965. After that date, they are to be restricted to the outer six miles.

As the law stood, previous to the Convention, foreigners were able to fish right up to three miles from the shore, but certain other countries, such as Iceland, claimed up to twelve miles of their coastal waters.

The matter was further aggravated by the fact that our deep-sea people, quite rightly, are tied down to a minimum-sized mesh, also to the size of the fish landed. As all is grist to the foreigner's mill, he seemed to please himself. With his small meshes, he swept up immatures by the million, quite useless on the food market and only of interest to the meal and manure processors.

A great friend of mine, Mr. Jack Williams, who owned a couple of seiner trawlers fishing out of Conway, brought this murderous practice home to the Lancashire and Western Sea Fisheries Committee when he showed a colour film of two fish-full cod ends coming aboard. First, there was his own catch in a net of regulation size where the fish, as they came alongside, were recognisable through the mesh. This was followed by a shot of a Frenchman hauling in the vicinity. The meshes were so small that the bulky contents could not even be seen.

Chapter 15

About Other Shellfish

Dublin Bay Prawns

THIS species has been rather mis-named, for it is not like the prawn as we know it. It is also known as Norwegian Lobster, or more popularly as Scampi—and to the scientists by the rather horrible title Nephrops.

Apart from being in at the catching and eating of them in the Mediterranean and Ireland, I have little first-hand knowledge, so will have to fall back on extracts from a paper by Mr. Colom O'Reardon of the Irish Fisheries Department, published by the Royal Dublin Society, Balls Bridge, Dublin. There is an immense amount of meat in this report, but space allows for only the following brief extraction:

"The distribution of Nephrops Norvegicus, the Dublin Bay prawn or Norway Lobster, is widespread in European waters. It occurs in the Mediterranean, off the south and west costs of Portugal, in the Gulf of Gascony, as well as around the coasts of Great Britain, and Ireland; in the North Sea, Kattegat and Skagerak, off the Faroes and the southern coast of Iceland. It has been recorded from depths of 17 to 600 metres, though it is more commonly taken in waters of 30 m. to 200 m., and it appears to have a wide adaptability to temperature and salinity as shown by its presence in the Baltic and Mediterranean.

"The term 'Dublin Bay Prawn' probably originated from the practice of the Dublin deep-sea trawlermen of earlier years shooting their gear off the Lambay Deep on their return journey to the port. The resulting catch of prawns which came to be regarded as a perquisite of the crews would thus be alive and fresh when unloaded in Dublin. There is, however, no evidence to show that the species was present to any extent in Dublin Bay itself.

"Nephrops are actively fished from April to September. Early in the period 1951 to 1962 peak landings occurred late in season, i.e., August or September, though in recent years peak landings tend to occur earlier. In 1962 a number of vessels commenced fishing in March and the peak landings occurred in May and June. It is quite likely that the extension of the season has affected the peak landing month accordingly.

"Commercial fishing takes place mainly from the 15- to 30-fathom grounds in the south-west between Lambay and Clogher Head. Twenty-five to thirty 50-60-ft. boats engage in the fishing and the main landing places are Clogher Head, Balbriggan, Skerries and Howth. The bottom consists of soft mud, or mud and fine sand.

"In September, a considerable proportion of the females is ovigerous i.e., in berry or carrying their eggs. These eggs are greenish black at this period, being newly deposited. The proportion of females, berried or otherwise, in the catch declines rapidly as winter advances. By April, the eggs have developed a pinkish colour and are at the 'eyed' stage, i.e., ready to be hatched and cast off. This occurs during the latter half of April and early May and the planktonic stages of the newly hatched larval Nephrops swim in the upper layers of the sea for about three weeks, after which they take to the sea bottom and there undergo rapid moults with fast-increasing growth rate. When they reach the adult stage, moulting as a rule occurs most frequently during the periods April-May and August-September. The proportion of females in the catch increases during the late April to early September period, often reaching a maximum of over 50 per cent during June and July. In the winter months the proportion of females present is low, reaching a minimum in the January and February period. Females have a considerably lower mean average length; consequently, the great reduction in the number of females present during the winter months could be the reason why there is a tendency for the mean length of the winter samples to rise somewhat.

"In recent years there has been a growing commercial demand for Nephrops, the tails (marketable portion) of which are generally more than 2 in. long (Plate XXV). This corresponds to a carapace length of 2.7 cm. (8.8 cm. total length). Individuals with a carapace length of not less than 3.4 cm. (11.0 cm. total length) are considered to be of prime quality.

This figure can be used as a convenient yardstick to evaluate the 'market quality' of samples of Nephrops.

"The main fishery is by sizeable trawlers, but a breakthrough that will be of interest to lobstermen is taking place off the north western coast of Scotland. According to a report in 'Fishing News' of November 13th, 1964, this pot fishery is paying fair dividends.

"It runs 'Any seaward areas of soft mud might well be worth investigating.

" 'Special prawn traps are each catching an easy £1 a week for the fishing vessel *Sweet Home* off Skye (Plate XXVI). Mr. William Finlayson and his crew have been experimenting with various types of adapted Leakey lobster traps with the result that large prawns to the value of 4s to 5s. a trap are taken at each lift. They are being fished within a mile or two off-shore in 30–40 fathoms, and although they can be caught at much shallower depths, there is the added nuisance of crabs entering the traps.

" 'The prawns, all large, averaging nine tails to the pound, are caught at the rate of five to seven a trap on average and at the processing factory at Stornoway, they fetch £6 a stone—nearly 1s. a prawn. The special traps, a modification of the East Coast lobster creel, are used. These, made by R. and B. Leakey of Settle, Yorkshire, should recover their cost, of around 45s., in about a couple of weeks.

" 'Experiments are continuing to increase the number the creels will take at one time. Although this appears to be governed more by the distribution of prawns on the sea floor and their range of foraging rather than by the design of creels. Very nearly as many were caught when the creels were lifted after a few hours as when lifted daily, and the number nearly doubled when lifted after two days. Only a very small piece of bait is taken by each prawn.

"Besides having a small mesh netting, the creels are lightweight, yet designed to sink quickly and settle right way up. Wood floored creels, when tried, proved unsuccessful, and it is assumed this was because they did not always land flat, and sank into the soft mud in which prawns live. The special traps have the two eyes of conventional creels, with galvanised steel frames, and in the conditions being worked, the sea damage is negligible; it is anticipated they will last many years. A special feature is the end door which enables the catch to be poured out on release of a toggle, resulting in rapid handling.'

"*Sweet Home's* crew of three, who were inexperienced in this type of fishing, found no difficulty in working 220 creels in 2½ hours, and anticipate even greater speeds with improved deck gear. Spaced at eight to 10 fathoms along the 'trot' or back rope, the light weight of these creels (around 10 lb.) is a big advantage when a number are suspended above the sea floor at one time when fishing at, say, 60-fathom depths!

"'Nephrop prawns evidently live in colonies, and prefer mud of "sticky" consistency at any depth. They live in holes in the mud, and evidently use it as a refuge when danger threatens. Hitherto, they have been caught round our coasts in trawl nets which have a comparatively thin wire rope as foot-rope which is designed to sink into the mud and lift them into the net. Fishermen using these trawls have noted that the best catches usually occur at dawn and often again at dusk, which means that at other times they are in their burrows, since it is hardly likely that they are fast enough to escape a trawl when on the surface. Discussing this point with Mr. Leakey, who has seen the working of these trawls under water as a skin diver, our correspondent was told that it seemed highly probable that for every box of prawns landed by trawls there must be many more boxes of prawns, particularly small ones, destroyed by being squashed and suffocated in the mud beneath the trawl.

"'Mr. Leakey knows of no research into the damage done to uncaught prawns by trawling, and remarked that if evidence of over-fishing of prawn grounds had not already become evident, it is probably because of the large size of these grounds, and in view of the disastrous future consequences of such trawling, if it does in fact destroy uncaught prawns, it is most urgent that the fact should be investigated scientifically. He hopes that this break-through of catching with traps will point the way to conservation.

"'According to scientists at the Torry laboratory at Aberdeen, the reason why prawns in the South Minch are so large, compared with those caught on more exposed grounds, is because they are not preyed on so extensively by open sea predators, particularly cod. This is good news for fishermen who have prawn mud in lochs and bays where cod are less common, and the West coast of Scotland in particular has many such places inside the three-mile limit where trawling is prohibited. Such grounds deserve investigation with traps and might provide lucrative fishing as the market is large and unsatisfied.

"'Fishing them with these traps is easy. They take any bait—salt mackerel or herring, conger, dog fish and even prawn bodies after the tails have been removed—and they eat very little of the bait, leaving the rest intact. It pays to try many places when searching for them, but one curious fact is that no small prawns were caught by *Sweet Home* even with fine mesh traps. Sometimes females predominate in the catch, suggesting there is segregation of sex and size in the colonies.'

"Scientists tell us the size of Nephrop prawns is governed by the degree to which they are preyed upon by cod, and also by the fishing effort to which they are subjected. It is logical therefore to assume that colonies of large prawns exist on all deeper rough ground wherever the mud is not scoured away by strong currents. Rough ground not only shelters pockets of the mud they like, but could also shelter the prawns from marauding cod. If such ground is trawled at all, it is by trawls with large bobbins that don't easily catch prawns. The only way to be sure there are not lucrative colonies of large prawns on your local rocky sea floor areas, is to fish them with prawn traps. If there are no prawns, the traps will be useful for lobster and crab."

Bear in mind the prices mentioned in that report are a few years out of date now and current rewards will be much higher.

From a gourmet viewpoint the deep frozen and rather taste-less tails dished up in this country cannot hold a candle to the freshly-boiled whole "Scampi" one gets abroad. And so often in this country they are further ruined by frying in some substitute oil that did not spring from the loins of an olive tree.

The Common Prawn

Although this book is mostly about the larger creepers and crawlers of the sea bottom, it might be as well to include a little about that tasty morsel the prawn. I say "tasty" but in my opinion it is less of a palate-tickler than a freshly cooked brown shrimp, preferably eaten out of a paper bag while perambulating the Promenade at Morecambe. Both, in my opinion, are ruined, in common with most food, by deep freezing.

153

Generally speaking, prawns inhabit the same sort of bottom as lobsters but at lesser depths. Both also must have overhead cover to survive, be it stones or weed, with the accent on the latter for prawns. There are three professional methods of capture.

Trawling

The possibility of using this method will depend on the ground to be worked. Most productive areas are those where eelgrass grows. "Eel" is a misnomer, as it looks very much like ordinary broad-leafed grass. I have tried trawling in a small way with a beam-type shrimp trawl, but retired from the fray when it was found that my grassy area had too many foot rope snags. Catches between snag tangling were fair but were not sufficient for commercial purposes.

Prawn Potting and Ring Netting

I cannot do better than quote from Alec Gibson's "Prawn Fishing", published by his Department in Dublin. I have permission also to include the rather funny little informative sketch of operating hoop nets (Fig. 24). I particularly like the set of the flat-hatted oarsman's scarf! Also the length of the one-armed operator's arm.

Pot or Creel Fishing

This method of prawning, like that by the hoop-net described later on, can, unlike trawling, be carried on as a part-time occupation which allows a fisherman to engage in other forms of fishing and other work generally. Creels made of close-woven wicker work, and shaped like miniature lobster creels, have now been largely superseded by square or rectangular wire framed mesh-covered pots and similarly constructed creels. Both pots and creels are most efficiently fished in groups or trots. Each trot usually consists of a dozen pots or creels which are attached at three- or four-fathom intervals to a bottom rope. It is a wise precaution to anchor both ends of the trot rope when fishing on exposed shores, though it is unnecessary to do so in quiet inlets. A buoy-line is attached to one or both ends of the trot rope. It is also a wise precaution to attach the buoy-line with a swivel to the trot line anchor, where strong tides run, in order to avoid fouling and consequent shortening of the buoy-line. A commercial fleet of pots or creels usually comprises between 6 and 8 trots, for which a boat of at least 20 ft. is required, if the fleet is to be handled with comfort. The design of a prawn creel is shown in Fig. 25. The creel rather than the pot is described in this figure, because it was found by experiment in Irish waters that the

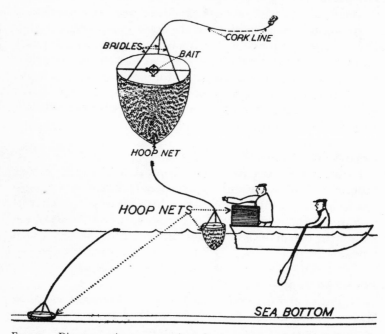

FIG. 24. Diagrammatic representation of a hoop net, and method of stowing and shooting hoop-nets from a small craft. (Leaflet No. 3, Dept. of Lands Fisheries Division, Dublin)

creel is slightly more efficient than the pot. It is imperative that the mesh covering the creel frame must not be greater than $\frac{3}{8}$-in. in diameter. If the mesh is smaller, say $\frac{1}{4}$ in. it will be found to capture the tiny prawns, which will cause difficulties when the catch is being handled and sorted. Furthermore, there is a tendency, with too small a mesh, towards reduced catches of marketable prawns.

The typical ground where prawns are found is on the sand

and mud patches of the foreshore between rock outcrops and surrounded by the large oarweed at low water mark. Prawns will also be found commonly where eelgrass is re-appearing. It is advisable to fish creels as near the large oarweeds as possible, without their being covered by them. If creels are fished every four hours from dawn to dusk, it will be found that the catches during the hours of daylight are poor and that best returns are obtained at or before dawn and at or after dusk. For this reason it will be found economical to set the creels in late evening, pick them up shortly after dark, reset them on the same grounds and fish them again preferably just before dawn. After dawn fishing the creels are normally taken ashore for cleaning and rebaiting.

The most successful bait appears to be crushed green shore-crab. It is relatively easy to capture large quantities of shore crabs by baiting with waste fish an old lobster pot to which a smaller eye has been fixed, or some similar kind of trap. If the baited trap is placed amongst the brown sea-weeds of the middle shore-line, large quantities of green crabs are likely to be captured, the quantity depending, of course, on the state of the tides. The bait crab should be crushed in order to expose the coral and meats of the legs. Overcrushing should be avoided because the best of the bait may be washed out of the creel when setting. Other successful baits include salt-herring and gurnard, flat-fish heads, limpets and mussels. None of these, however, has been found to be as good as green crab.

The crushed crab, or other small bait, can either be tied in a shrimp-net bag and suspended from the eye in the upright in the middle of the creel (Fig. 25) or broadcast on the floor of the creel. The confinement of the bait in a bag has the advantage of allowing it to be used at least twice, and thus avoids much re-baiting. On the other hand, there are grounds for stating that when the bait is broadcast on the bottom of the creel larger catches of prawns are likely.

Hoop-net

The hoop-net is constructed from a light metal or wire hoop, 3 ft. in diameter, to which a cone-shaped shrimp netting bag is lashed. The depth of the bag should not exceed 3 ft. Each hoop-net has 3 bridles which meet to form a buoy-line of the length required to fish the nets in not more than 5 fathoms of water.

156

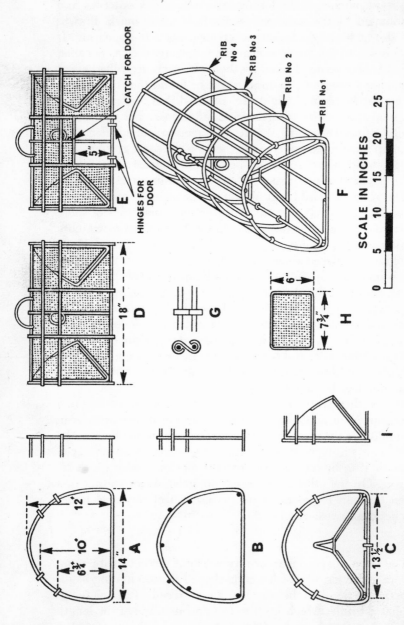

Fig. 25. Diagram of the construction of a prawn creel. A—ribs Nos. 1 & 4. B—ribs Nos. 2 & 3. C—end view showing lead in. D—elevation left side. E—elevation right side. F—isometric drawing entire creel. G—plan and elevation of hinge. H—door. I—detailed side view of entrance and rib No. 1. (From *Prawn Fishing*, Dept. of Lands, Fisheries Division, Dublin.)

Across the diameter of the hoop-net a baiting string is attached to which salt herring, gurnard, plaice heads, etc., are secured by a slip-knot. The advantages of the hoop-net are (1) cheapness and (2) the number of nets which can be carried. A small row-boat will take up to 50 hoop-nets, stowed one on top of the other on the stern sheet. When each net has been baited prior to setting out for the grounds it is laid upside down with the corks and buoy-line underneath. This greatly facilitates shooting a large number of hoop-nets stacked one on top of another. Hoop-nets are best fished on the same type of ground mentioned for creels, usually at or after dusk. Each hoop-net should be shot four to six fathoms apart. When the last net has been shot, the first one can be picked up. Each net need only be left fishing for a period of 10–20 minutes. Taking up the buoy-line, the net must be raised with great care off the bottom, and, when a fathom or so of the line is boarded, the remainder of it should be hauled in as rapidly as possible. More than one fishing can be made each night, though this and the extent of the catch will depend upon the clemency of the weather.

Here is a hoop netting tip I picked up on the Mediterranean. There, they attach a few small-leafed sprigs to the inside bottom of the net. This offers inviting cover when prawns are on the bait and stops the upward escape jump when the net is lifted. In addition to the bait, usually crushed and netted sardine, the fisher-man rubs a small piece of sandstone on some hard and offensive-smelling cheese rind each time the ring is raised. In a minor way I had a shot at prawn potting. I fabricated pots from the smallest gauge galvanised garden wire netting available fixed on to box-like square steel frames, with a door top-side. Spouts—one in each side—were wire cylinders tapered from 4 in. to inner openings of about $1\frac{1}{4}$ in. For ballast I used a couple of hand-fuls of wet concrete dumped on the inside bottom. It was found in practice that the $\frac{1}{2}$-in. mesh allowed all but the very largest prawns to escape, so I hit on the idea of dumping the pot into hot sticky tar to which I had added some cement to give it body. It had the added advantage of preserving the wire as well as reducing the mesh size considerably. Catches, though gastro-nomically welcome, were not spectacular. Had the pots followed Gibson's design, the tale might well have been different.

Our interest in prawns did not extend beyond the table. My wife, highly skilled in the preparation of all sea food, found that she could get all the prawns she required for sauces and paella decoration, by slinging a pot out of the kitchen window, on to the rocks below our piled-out living quarters.

Scallops

In search of further sidelines, especially winter ones, it was decided to have a look for scallops, as I had heard that in the past, there was a good fishery within a few miles of my home port. Before buying the rather expensive gear needed, I asked the Lancashire and Western Sea Fisheries Committee if they, in conjunction with the Ministry, would carry out a dredging survey, which they readily undertook.

The dredge used was of advanced design, being the brain-child of Mr. Dick Baird, who superintended the operation. To make it hug the bottom, a sizeable metal sheet, set at an angle to cause downward thrust was used, and the digging teeth were adjustable to allow different types of bottom to be searched.

After a few days of dredging with rather thin results, Baird's advice was "they are there, but not in commercial quantities—forget 'em". Later on, I had the good fortune to see Baird's underwater movie. One part of it showed a scallop taking flight from an on-creeping enemy, a starfish. By means of its jet propulsion, it winged surfacewards and went through the gyrations of a water-borne ballet dancer.

One interesting point did come to light, and that was that each scallop caught was a five-year-old. Scallops are known to live up to a dozen years, and their age can be accurately determined by counting the growth rings on the outer shell.

For those who would like to know more about this attractive sea food, I would recommend the reading of two pamphlets by Alec Gibson, "Escallops in Irish Waters", Royal Dublin Society, Balls Bridge, Dublin, and "Underwater Observations on Scallop Beds", published by the Irish Dept. of Fisheries, Dublin.

Mussels

The spread of Continental holidays is no doubt the reason for the upswing in appreciation of this most delectable morsel, whether it be eaten raw, oyster fashion, or included in dishes ranging from stews to curries. Possibly, it is at its best in a Moules Mariniere, the preparation of which will be dealt with later on.

The mussel is a creature of marked likes and dislikes with regard to its habitat and feeding, and a case in point is the success of beds at Portmadoc in North Wales, where for some reason it fattens to perfection. Unfortunately, however, the spat, or seed, will not hold on the bottom. This may be due to the violently scouring action of the freshets that tear down from the Snowdonian range of mountains, which usually occurs in summer when the mussel is busy reproducing itself. The result is that spat is washed seaward and buried in the shifting sand banks of the estuary.

To keep up the stock it is necessary to re-seed the beds with immatures that originate from places as far afield as the Lancashire coast.

Demand is such that machinery has had to be called in, and the mechanised process at Portmadoc begins with a Baird-designed dredge. Mussels and their accompanying rubbish are dumped directly into the dredger's hold, and later cleared by a mobile crane on the quayside.

From the quayside the catch is transferred to power-driven screens for grading and washing by pressure jets. Rubbish and immatures fall through, and are put aboard another craft for transfer back to the beds. Meanwhile, the selected mussels pass on to the cleansing tanks where they undergo a process of self-cleaning in sterilised seawater for 48 hours. Finally, they are bagged and closed with the official seal, denoting purity (Plate XXIII).

On the mechanics of sterilisation from polluted areas, I cannot do better than quote from Alec Gibson's "Storage of Shellfish", which relates to preparation for retail marketing.

Incidentally, mussels for cooking by processors may be sent direct, side-slipping the purification tanks, as the high temperature cooking method employed kills all the bugs. Alec Gibson has this to say on sterilisation:

"Mussels, cockles and oysters may be purified by operating a relatively simple tank technique. For this purpose it is essential to have cement-rendered tanks. The dimensions of these tanks are largely a matter of choice. Baird recommends three tanks measuring 5 ft. 6 in. by 6 ft. 6 in. by 1 ft. 6 in. in depth, with a capacity of 297 gallons each for the serving of which a water-storage tank containing about 2,000 gallons is required.

"In each treatment tank, wooden slotted grids are placed on the bottom, leaving just enough space at the edges so that they may be easily lifted. The grids serve the function of allowing the waste products of the shell-fish, viz., sand, mud, excreta, shell chippings etc., to fall to the bottom, where they will not come into contact with the shell-fish again and can be hosed away subsequent to treatment.

"A 1½-in. centrifugal pump is sufficient to fill the storage tank for this number of tanks. The storage tank is at a higher level than the treatment tanks which are fed from it by gravity. The outlets from the treatment tanks should be at least 6-in. porcelain pipes, so that all the sediment can be freely washed out of the tanks. The procedure to be adopted for purifying the shell-fish is briefly as follows. The storage tank is filled with water and sterilised by adding chlorine at the rate of 3 parts per million of sea-water, and allowing it to stand for 12 hours. The chlorine is then neutralised by adding sodium thiosulphate (Hypo). The shell-fish are immersed in this sterilised and chlorine free water, and having lain in it for 24 hours are hosed down with sterilised seawater to remove excess wastes. The process is then repeated in a second bath of seawater sterilised in exactly the same way. The shell-fish function normally in the sterilised water, with the result that they filter out of their system any waste products likely to contain harmful matter. At the end of the second bath the shellfish are bathed with chlorinated but not neutralised seawater. This causes them to close their shells and cease to function, so that the shells themselves become sterilised. Thus, both the insides and the outsides of the shell-fish are sterilised. Each bath in sterilized seawater should continue for 24 hours and the final, chlorine only treatment for sterilising the shells should last for 2 hours.

"The most convenient method of mixing the commercial chlorine with the storage tank water is to allow it to drip steadily on the inflowing seawater passing from the storage tank into the chlorination tank. In order to make certain of neutralising all the chlorine in the water, before it enters the treatment tanks it is necessary to make up a solution of Hypo at the rate of one pound to a gallon of water. Three-quarters of a pint of this solution will be sufficient to neutralise the chlorine in each 100 gallons of water. The Hypo is most efficiently mixed with the sterilised water by allowing it to drip steadily into the water flowing from the chlorination tank to the treatment tanks. It is advisable to take the water supply for the storage tank at high tide when there is every chance that clean well-aerated water will be available. The shell-fish must be scrubbed free of excess mud, sand, barnacles, chippings, etc., and well hosed down before being placed in the tanks."

The demand for mussels on the British market cannot so far be met, and processors have to rely too much on Dutch and Danish imports, which is a pity, as mussels seem to be in inexhaustible quantities around our coasts. But to bring them to marketable prefection it is necessary, in most cases, to move them from their crowded sea beds, where the competition for food is too great, to the quieter estuaries where maximum water coverage and good feeding conditions can be found.

Oysters

A chilly wind of change has blown over our oyster beds. A hundred years ago Sam Weller was able to declare "It's a werry wemarkable circumstance, Sir, that poverty and oysters always seem to go together". In those days they were pence a long hundred. During the first World War, I enjoyed river Roach natives at 3s. 6d. a hundred, opened for me by a smacksman for a share of my Guinness. Today, that expenditure might buy three over the oyster bar. Hereabouts in Caernarvon Bay in Sam Weller's day there was a huge sea oyster fishery, but today nothing remains on the beds but dead shell. The reason for this is wrapped in mystery.

With the disappearance of the rough-shelled sea oyster, natives are being farmed with some success in rivers and estuaries around our coasts, the principal farming area being around Colchester.

Sexually, the oyster is an undecided creature much given to change of sex, which conjures up thoughts of high drama on the oyster beds at birthday time. They are reputed, when breeding, to hatch out as many as a million free-swimming children, which after about a couple of weeks' freedom attach themselves to a suitable clean surface. Mortality due to tidal action, gales and predators can be as high as 90 per cent. in their first year of life. Thereafter the remainder are lucky if they get away with an annual mortality of 20 per cent. for their remaining two or three years. Growth depends on feed which in turn depends on water temperature.

The Ministry of Agriculture and Fisheries are doing some excellent work on cutting these losses by breeding oysters in captivity. This is done in tanks in which are immersed lime and sand washed tiles that attract spat settlement. This, in due course, is scraped off prior to sowing on some selected bottom, where the young oysters are left to mature.

Whelks

Although whelks are normally dredged for in the shallows beyond the extreme low-water mark, they can be taken in fair quantities by means of pots.

As they are carnivorous, the bait is similar to that used in lobster and crawfishing; fish waste and other flesh being the best.

One must admire the whelk, even if only for its cleverness and ingenuity in getting a feed off a live bi-valve. Patiently, it waits alongside until the bi-valve's shell opens, and then with remarkable alacrity swings its own shell so that the lower lip comes between the opening, thus preventing the two halves from closing tight. It then inserts its proboscis and the poor victim becomes the main dish of the day.

Although the flesh of the whelk is tough and rubbery, it can, with plenty of cooking and served in chilli vinegar, become palatable, and for those who like this shellfish and who wish to catch their own, I give here a step by step guide of a method of constructing whelk pots which appeared long ago in "Fishing News". It is a remarkably sturdy pot, and the details for constructing such a contraption have always fascinated me (Fig. 26).

The base of the pot consists of a circular metal plate about 18 in. in diameter, drilled at equal distances around the rim with eight holes. Into these holes are welded metal rods which are then bowed slightly to be welded at the top to a metal ring about six to eight inches in diameter. This now gives a shape similar to an open umbrella frame without the handle.

Bend on to one of the rods a piece of rope, and taking it round the rod opposite, fasten the other end to the first rod. This gives two parallel lines running across the centre of the pot between which is placed the bait. To hold the bait securely, either metal or rope rings are drawn along the parallel lines towards the bait, thus tightening it between the lines (don't forget to put these on to the rope before making it fast!).

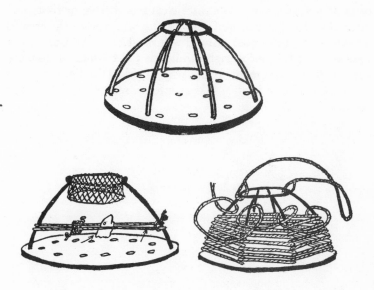

FIG. 26.   Stages in constructing a whelk pot

About twelve fathoms of rope which has been well used for buoys or mooring is now required to fill in the framework. Used rope is a must for this, as whelks shy away from anything as rough as new rope.

Bend one end of the rope on to the base of one of the metal rods, and working in a clockwise direction, take a simple, but tight, turn around each of the other rods. Continue layer upon layer until the whole framework is covered, hammering the rope down hard on to the layer below.

A piece of netting secured around the top ring and hanging to a depth of two or three inches acts as an excellent escape inhibitor.

The mooring rope is attached by means of a rope handle spliced on to the top ring, and as it is essential to haul the pot in an upright position, to prevent the contents from being tipped out, ensure that the handle is well balanced.

A few holes drilled in the base plate will help drainage when hauling—but watch the size of these.

There are, of course, one or two variations in the construction of these pots, such as hoop bases with metal slats, or rope, but one has to decide for oneself which is the best type for the area to be fished. A strong tidal ground will need the weight of a solid base to keep the pot upright while on the bottom, but where there is little movement in the way of tides, the lighter pot is obviously the best choice, taking into account the problems of hauling and handling.

Chapter 16

Choice of Craft

CHOICE of craft for a lobster fishery will depend on the grounds to be worked and the number of pots to be fished. When considering design it is well to take into account the fact that the vessel might, in addition to potting, be used for other types of fishing and ploys.

These might include trawling, trammeling, lining, and drifting, and, who knows, there may be pennies from heaven in the form of salvage work? All of these things can occur in or out of the lobster season. A fishing boat is a machine and to pay for itself, and its upkeep, it must be kept working to full capacity.

Craft engaged in crawfishing come in various shapes and sizes. At the lower end of the scale are outboard powered dinghies, or in Ireland, canvas covered curraghs propelled by rowing sticks, which are run as a sideline by coastal crofters and usually fish at most a couple of dozen pots. At the other end of the scale is a 75 footer I met in Las Palmas. She was out of Camaret in France, engaged in craw fishing the deep and virgin grounds between the Canaries and the West African coast.

Her skipper/owner told me that he favoured the continuous fishing method, and that he set between 400 and 500 pots, at depths of up to 50 fathoms, at a time. The crew numbered four and they were absent from their home port from December until May. Catches were sold on the local market at good prices. Towards the end of his stay he filled his circulation tanks and took the catch back to France, where he attracted even better returns.

I started my apprenticeship with Twm, in a fairly easily pulled 16 footer, with a small rag of a mizzen that kept her head up when working and to some extent made use of the wind when it was in a "soldierly" direction. Propulsion was of course, by "Armstrong's Patent". Twm's oars of springy ash were beautifully balanced by running lead into the inner extremities. Blades were narrow and sticklike—obviously the Irish influence.

During my fishing years I have had five boats, three too small, one too big and the fifth, to which I gave a good deal of design thought, fulfilled all my expectations.

Lotus V (Plate III on page 66), for that is her name, has an overall of 20 ft., a beam of 8 ft. and an after draught of 2 ft. 3 in. She was built by Crossfields of Conway. Her planking was of 1 in. hill-grown larch on grown frames of Welsh oak at 10 in. centres and doubled to the turn of the bilge. The forrard and after decks were short and sunk about six in. below the gun-wale to act as safe storage shelves for odds and ends of gear. She was found to be rather heavy on the helm due to her large rudder, but this was easily rectified by fitting a balancing blade ahead of the rudder axis. What varnished brightwork she had was of teak, as I have a horror of the bastard mahogany known as West African, which is prone to discolouration under varnish and rots at the end grain if exposed to weather. Under several coats of paint, however, some of it behaves reasonably well.

While she was being built each piece of timber, other than teak, was soaked in "Cuprinol" as a rot preventative.

Teething troubles were limited to the power unit, a 9 hp petrol Kelvin Ricardo. Nothing at all wrong with the engine, but the ignition was completely haywire in more ways than one. This apparently was caused by faulty post-war (it was 1947) winding wire that broke down with the merest hint of internal condensation. Lucas, the makers, were very good and sent one of their backroom boys down with instructions to go to sea with us until the gremlin of condensation had been defeated. Apart from the faulty winding wire, it was found that Lucas had so concentrated on water-proofing the magneto that it was impossible for the condensation to dry out. We found the answer to be a very simple one. We drilled a half-inch hole in the base so that damp air could get in, and what is more important, out.

We ran this engine on petrol rather than petrol/paraffin because of the danger of failure and subsequent difficulty in starting while working close inshore.

Later on, and for no particular reason, I put some salvage money into a 10 hp A.V. 2 Petter. Knowing little about the ease of starting small diesels, I included electrics. All went well for several years until the starter bendix stuck and I had to hand start. This, in fact, proved so easy, that since then the bendix has been allowed to lie, and electrics relegated to operating a cigarette lighter.

Originally, a useful little mizzen was fitted, but I was able to dispense with this when I built a steering shelter right forrard. With this, I found *Lotus V* would heave to comfortably nearly stern on. The shelter was particularly comforting when on passage to and from the grounds. One just opens the throttle in practically any weather and allows the spray and dollops of green water to come over the top. This would, of course, have been impossible with an electrically-ignited engine, however well housed.

Incidentally, the teak used in constructing the shelter came from the foredeck of HMS *Conway*—the vessel that came to such an ignominious end in the swillies of the Menai Straits.

In spite of her full bow sections, *Lotus V*, when working in confused tidal race conditions, where seas came at her from every angle, was inclined occasionally to dip her stem. To overcome this, and on the advice of an aircraft designer, a couple of tapered fins were fitted just above the boot topping which extended some 6 ft. aft from the stern. They were approximately quarter round in section, tapering gently fore and aft from a 4 in. centre. The flat, or slightly upwards-tilted underside checked the plunge and the rounded top allowed water to escape easily on the recovery upswing. They also flattened out the spray and made for comfort at the tiller.

Inshore working may well be accompanied by many rocky touchdowns and as contact invariably occurs at the place of maximum draught, that is, aft, at the propeller-protecting heel, or skeg, some form of shock absorbing protection is required. After a few teeth-shattering bumps, I fabricated a protecting 6 ft. long shoe with an inch thick sole and half inch sides and fixed this by bolting it right through the keel. Any future teeth-shattering was accompanied by the easy thought that the shoe and not the timber was absorbing the shock.

Should you decide to have a new vessel, the ideal, of course, is to build to the requirements of the job, and if you or your partner has a background of inshore fishing you may get some really helpful financial and practical assistance under the White Fish Authority's scheme for grants and loans, details of which can be obtained from the Secretary, White Fish Authority,

Lincoln's Inn Chambers, 2/3 Cursitor Street, London, E.C.4.

On the other hand, should you decide to look around for a secondhand craft, good luck to you, but there are many snags. Unless you have intimate knowledge of construction, money will be well spent on a competent survey, but carry out a preliminary examination before you arrange to have her looked over professionally.

Stand well back and look for loss of shape—she may be hogged. By this, I mean a slight humping of the sheer line. If so, walk away, and keep on walking, for she is beyond human endeavour. This point cleared up, start at the keel and prod all the planking with a sharp knife, including stern and transom. If any soft parts are found, mark with chalk and later find out whether they are worth replacing. Inside the vessel, treat all planking and timbers in the same way, paying special attention to both ends of the vessel and timber condition behind the lockers.

A place particularly prone to rot, due to weeps of wet from the deck covering board, is the shelf area. By "shelf" I mean the joints between deck beams and hull. If the craft has a fish well, pay special attention to the deck above it. Do not worry about any vertical shakes in the spars, but be wary of any transverse hair lines. They are a certain indication of future fracture. Have a look at any standing rigging and if doubtful cast off a seizing and look for corrosion or broken wires.

Canvas, if any, should be opened out and the stitching checked for weakness and material tested for "sickness". This is done simply by inserting a sharp spike at various points. If on withdrawing the spike the weave does not jump back into its original shape, it indicates that its useful life is drawing to a close.

This, of course, is only part of the professional survey tale, but if carried out it will at least save the survey fee on possibly a good-looking and well painted boat that is suffering internally. One more tip. Get your nose to work when opening up cabin and lockers. A wrong 'un invariably smells mustily sick.

Gear

The most easily lost thing on my boat is the rough knife sharpener or gritstone. I managed to defeat this delinquent by bolting a round carborundum wheel across the flat of the capstan head. As this item is a permanent fixture, and usually running, it is only necessary to give the knife an occasional wipe to attain the sharp but rather rough edge necessary for cutting up bait. I also carry an axe for the reduction of sheep heads to sizeable proportions. It is also useful in dealing with the occasional snarl-up.

I bought my knives on Fleetwood Fish Dock, and the more they wear down the more I like them, especially for gutting. Filleting is usually done for home consumption, and for this I use a worn down and whippy old steel carving knife—a tip I got from an old lady hawking flounders on the Lancashire coast.

Most of the bait was cut up ashore, and one of my most treasured possessions was a small slab of gritstone given to me by an old gipsy clothes-peg maker, in return for a small service rendered. He told me that it came from "somewhere south of the Cotswolds" and that the actual location of the stony bonanza was known only to the "peggers".

For good value, he also taught me how to make pegs with an old steel table knife, ground to a most peculiar shape.

Another useful tool is the baiting needle (Fig. 27(a)). Usually, the jamming string method is used in baiting a pot, but in certain types I found the bait lasted longer if the flesh, and if possible, a bit of bone, were punctured and twine passed through. This is simply achieved by threading the baiting needle with binder twine and pushing it through, leaving two loose ends with which to secure the bait. It was found to work very well on Cornish and French-type pots.

Without doubt, the most important tool on board is the float recovery gaff (Fig. 27(b)). After experimenting with various types, I settled for one made of $\frac{3}{8}$ in. round steel, with a length of three feet. One end I let into a large file handle and the other was widely hooked.

The first one I made promptly sank when dropped overboard accidentally, so I fixed three corks to just below the handle of the second model. This one floated beautifully—and frequently —and was easily retrieved.

For recovering floats which have drifted into inaccessible inshore positions, during on-shore blows, we carry a long hooked gaff made up of two stowable lengths of bamboo, connected by a brass ferrule.

We have yet another useful tool on board which has more than once got us out of dire trouble and prevented a stranding.

It is used when we have the misfortune to foul a pot float line, which more often than not belongs to someone else. Before the

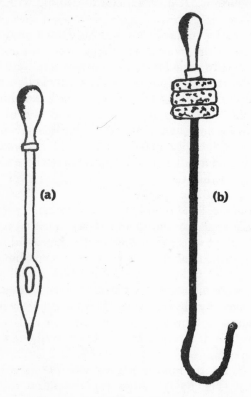

(a)   (b)

FIG. 27.   (a) baiting needle.   (b) pot gaff

engine can be put into neutral, the rope has invariably got itself into a few over-tight jamming turns around the shaft between the propeller boss and stern tube, and the only answer, if close inshore, is to quickly chuck out the anchor. Our 20 lb. C.Q.R. is always kept at the "ready" position on the fore deck for this very reason.

To extricate ourselves from this predicament, we first try to unravel the tangle by placing the engine in reverse and winding by hand to see if the rope will free itself. This seldom happens, so it is usually a case of bringing the pot on board, looking around for a tow home, or going overside with a knife.

The latter solution is fine on a hot summer's day, but there are too few of these, so after a couple of bone-chilling dives we devised an instrument which makes short work of destroying a rope. Into an ash broomstick a rough piece of saw-blade is riveted, and with this it is usually possible to worry and tear the recalcitrant turns free, without getting immersed.

Although usually small and compact, a fishing vessel is a marvellous place for losing the small objects of gear which should be readily to hand and quickly recognisable. Painted a bright fluorescent red, however, they can usually be spotted fairly quickly.

Fluorescent material comes in useful for dahn or marker flags, which in the past were always of black canvas. The new ones can be seen at far greater distances in most lights, except only at dawn and dusk.

For floats, I gradually changed over to plastic, which doesn't waterlog like cork, and is not so prone to weed growth. Also, it floats better—which is an important point if there is a tide running.

About weed growth on pots and lines. There is always a small proportion of our pots and lines drying out ashore, where a couple of sunny days puts paid to any weed growth and allows the pots to sweeten.

A stinking, slimy pot, strangely enough, repels the lobster, so fishing time is not wasted while being dried out in this way. I think the fact that the lobster is repelled is strange because lobsters don't seem to mind stinking food. In fact, in my experience that is the way they prefer it.

One of the advantages of using tangy bait is that one is not worried by crabs, congers and dogfish, who only go for "oven-ready", fresh bait.

Another gadget that has proved its worth many times is a small grappling hook. By using it, it is sometimes possible to retrieve lost gear. Ours consists of three pieces of $\frac{3}{8}$ in. rod, bent in the form of large hooks. These were welded together and attached to about a fathom of chain, which acted as a sinker. A ring attachment allows a rope to be bent on. The whole thing is fairly light so that if it fouls on rough ground it is possible to free it with an oversize pull.

Crew

As this chapter has dealt with useful things to have about a boat, here are a few notes on my crewing problems. For the first two years on my own, I employed a handy school-leaving lad—the type that comes of really good stock. Although ham-fisted, he was thoroughly trustworthy, but unfortunately left me to go to sea.

By that time I was extending my range, and as I couldn't find another lad of his type, I tried employing a local man. He stayed with me for the lobster season, then swallowed the anchor. The reasons he gave me were that he disliked the irregular hours—anything up to eighteen per day—and he was sick of the battering he got from the sea. He said he would be more comfortable on the dole—and I must say I agreed with him!

Also around that time, I had the good fortune to marry a sea-keeping wife who worked like a Trojan and between us we kept the wheels turning for a year. My luck was still in and I found the ideal partner in the most excellent Huw, who came in with me on a fifty-fifty basis. He is one of the best, and always remains cucumber cool, whatever the emergency. During the considerable number of years we fished together, we were and still remain, exceedingly good friends. Our arrangement, of course, allowed "herself" to stay ashore and look after marketing and records.

Huw started lobstering at an early age with his father, but later decided to go to the South Wales coalpits where the dust got on his lungs. He wisely got out in time and returned home. He was a man of many skills, which ranged from upholstery to resuscitating the near-drowned. On one occasion he was standing in for a sick coastguard on rough weather watch, when he spotted a sailing dinghy in the front of an overland gale. It was apparently out of control, going seawards from the next bay. He knew that it hadn't a chance of survival, so he telephoned me to get under way and meet him *en route* from the watch hut. By this time the dinghy had capsized and was nowhere to be seen.

The course that Huw gave me was a masterpiece of navigation, as the dinghy suddenly appeared over our bows about two miles out. One of the crew was in good heart and was supporting his unconscious mate.

During the run for home, Huw got most of the water out of the "corpse" and immediately we beached, a little man in clerical garb jumped aboard in the hope of administering the last rites with his oil bottle. Huw, who was still working on the casualty, took a poor view of this, lost his temper and cursed the little man (a Catholic priest) to high heaven.

It was not until we had the body in a warm bed and put a medical shot into the arm that it opened its eyes.

His family, extremely rich, asked me how Huw could be rewarded, and I told them that a money gift was right out. Instead, I suggested a suitably inscribed silver cigarette case, and then, knowing their wealth, said they might as well make it gold.

The tail-piece to this true yarn was that—to everyone's disgust—nothing more was heard of my reasonable suggestion. Later on, news filtered through that the family had salved their conscience by installing a huge stained-glass window in their new church!

Keeping the Boat Working

As I have already mentioned, commercial fishing boats are machines, and should, subject to weather conditions, be put to maximum use, even to the extent of finding a use for them during the dark hours.

On one occasion, we made a most lucrative contract with the Atomic Energy people for a tidal survey. This, we thought, would mean that our gear would have to be brought ashore, but although it was the high lobster season, we were well covered, financially.

However, our idea of workable weather did not coincide with that of the boat-borne surveyor. Fortunately, he had a queasy stomach, so we were still able to work most of our gear, and get paid for the survey, despite the fact that not very much was done along those lines.

Occasionally, we have the good fortune to pick up a drifting derelict which had obviously broken its moorings. If it was not of local origin, we turned in tough salvage claims, which we considered "pennies from heaven".

On the other hand, of course, if there was a crewed boat in trouble, we did what we could to help, knowing that one day we might find ourselves in the same predicament.

But to return to the subject of dark night work. During the latter part of my apprenticeship with Twm, I heard a splashing commotion directly off our beach. This was reported to my master, whose reaction was "Drynogs" (Bass).

"Even if you had a seine net", he said, "there is no price in them." But being a tyro, I begged to differ, and went over to the Chester river and bought an old seine net. The first shot, a muddled and inexpert affair, netted no bass, but instead I found I had 75 lb. of salmon and sea trout averaging 4 lb. apiece. Salmon and sea trout spend most of their lives at sea, but I was surprised to get so many off an open beach, situated twenty miles distant from the nearest river's mouth.

This first catch naturally gave me ideas of untold wealth, but for the next week my after-dark toiling produced not one salmon. Later, I found the reason to be a combination of wrong weather conditions and the presence of a bright moon.

After much trial and error, I found the ideal conditions to be a light wind over the land to give a smart water ripple, a night as black as the inside of a cow, and the best time to be during the last two hours of flood—all preceded by a warm day that put the sand eels (the salmon's main diet) on the move.

Just for the record, I took one night a sizeable hen salmon, heavily in spawn. She was fit only for smoking, but the spawn (two full jam jars) gave me an idea. Ground baiting attracts the angler's fish, so why not mine? I scattered the spawn and trod it in between tide marks.

That night conditions were perfect when I hauled the net across the baited area, and although not one salmon was taken, the net was so loaded with bass—nearly a ton of them, as it turned out—I was unable to haul it ashore until the tide had ebbed.

I still have an open mind about ground baiting, but a marine biologist later gave me doubts when he told me that the bait had nothing to do with my catch, and that I had merely enclosed a "school".

These are just one or two ideas on working a boat to the full, but each area offers its own propositions—it's just a matter of keeping an eye open and using the grey matter.

Chapter 17

Hints on Trawling and Netting

O N my way homewards from Barrow and the sand fishery of Morecambe Bay, I called in to see a fisherman friend, Mr Jack Mount, and found both him and his wife sitting at a table piled high with boiled shrimps which they were picking for the processors. This is a highly skilled operation, and although I have tried many times, the art still eludes me.

Jack, a very active eighty plus, is a mine of information on fishing matters. He told me that his father used to base himself during the oyster season on my home port in Wales, working a large bank of oysters that no longer exists. Until he retired a couple of years ago, he was a nobby trawlerman, concentrating on shrimps and other fish in season.

Nobbys, "yacht-like" little craft, are between 30 and 40 feet in length. I put a foot wrong with Jack when I said "yacht-like".

"That be damned for a tale," he said, "Nobbys you know, have hardly altered in shape for the last hundred and fifty years. A hundred years ago gentlemen's yachts had clipper bows and in those days the old nobbys could sail rings round them."

To prove his point he told me to go and see Mr Fred Crossfield at Arnside who would show me a half model of a 50-foot nobby-built hull and spars, which cost £20 a hundred and fifty years ago. I just could not spoil his wrathful effusion by telling him that I had already yarned with Fred Crossfield and seen the half model. I must say that with the exception of a longer keel, the lines might well have come from the board of a designer of modern sea-going yachts. Jack told me that the old nobby men had three fevers which occurred in the following order: racing, fishing and strong drink. Fishermen left the building of hull and spars to the Crossfield family, but it was a point of honour for the nobby men to cut and sew their own sails.

Mechanical Shrimp Picker

Jack had some interesting news about a mechanical shrimp picker. It was of German origin, and was reputed to pick the smaller European shrimp. There are American machines on the market, but as their shrimps are considerably larger, their machines cannot handle our small variety. His Fisherman's Association, Morecambe Trawlers Ltd., imported the German machine. I did not see it in action, but gathered it worked by tipping the cooked shrimps into a revolving wire mesh drum with wire brushes turning counterwise on the outside, scratching

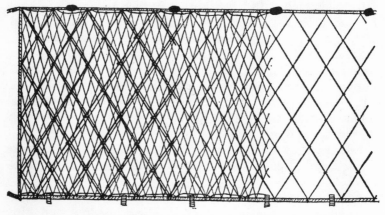

FIG. 28. Trammel net. "They are three nets in one—the walls of wide mesh with smaller, loosely hung inner mesh."

the shells adrift. He was not enthusiastic, and preferred the old method.

My next call was at Flint on the lower reaches of the Chester river. There I called on the Bithel family who had fished the river for generations by drifting their trammel nets (see Fig. 28) along the tidal gutters in search of salmon and fluke. In all probability, their forebears came over to this country in the reign of Queen Elizabeth I, who licensed Frenchmen to fish her rivers. With them they brought their "tres mailes" which can be roughly translated as "three meshes" which in time became known as trammels. An apt description, as they are three nets in one. Two walls are of very wide mesh about 10 inches knot to knot, with a smaller loosely hung inner mesh. The net works as a trap. Fish swimming into it go through the outer wall, strike the baggy inner mesh, and fall through the corresponding wall on the other side, which forms a holding bag. Before the introduction of nylon, which never seems to rot or disintegrate like the vegetable variety, I used to buy part-worn trammels from the Bithel family and use them as lobster nets. They were set on rough ground with pieces of bait tied at intervals along the cork-line. Lobsters trying to get at the bait managed to snarl themselves in the mesh and were held fast until they were extricated.

Shore Seine Net is Useful

Another useful tool for the inshoreman or part-timer, is a shore seine net. Perhaps the best way of explaining its operation is to describe my own experience with one. For some reason best known to himself, my old master Twm had no interest in netting salmon, although, in spite of the fact that we were 20 miles from the nearest salmon river, there were plenty, in season, along our shore-line.

The wife side of the team and I decided to try our luck and ordered a net 75 yards long, 12 feet deep in the centre tapering to 6 feet at the wing or shore ends. These ends were kept open by 6-foot spreaders or poles weighted at the bottom. The method was to place one of the spreaders with bridled rope attached across the dinghy sternboard, then carefully coil corks and leads either end of the board, placing the second spreader on top. This spreader was jerked off a few yards from the shore and the dinghy rowed quietly out and round in a semi-circle towards the shore. Both spreaders were pulled ashore together and taken a few yards up the beach and net hauled shorewards by cork and lead lines. Any fish would be either meshed in their struggles to escape, or trapped in the baggy middle of the net.

We were in such a hurry to try it out that immediately it arrived from the makers, Knox & Company of Kilbirnie, it was promptly rigged and as soon as darkness fell it was in the water. In our very first shot, rather a cock-eyed affair, we "grassed" amongst other fish fourteen salmon and sea trout weighing 75 lb. This was a bit of a problem as we had no £5 licence so the bull had to be taken by the horns. Most of the catch was laid out on a trailer and surrendered to a good friend of mine, James, the River Board bailiff, who was responsible for all salmon fishing, both coastal and river. He told me there were two courses open to him: first to seize the fish and let them rot pending a court case, or—here is where the judgment of Solomon came in— give me a licence in exchange for the fish, as his daughter ran a fish shop. This to us did not seem illegal, as the fish were caught after midnight and the licence was dated accordingly.

James, rest his soul, was a delightful companion and a keen fisherman. In his early days he was one of the most skilful poachers in Wales, until one day he mistimed an explosive charge, destined for a salmon pool, and blew his hand off, wrist high. The River Board, in their wisdom, then employed him, and his murderous-looking hook in lieu of a hand, in their service. That hook, which he sharpened, struck terror into later generations of wrongdoers.

Measuring Meshes

Before closing this section on shore netting, I will clarify mesh measurement, which is important where the law specifies a minimum size. For instance, a mesh consisting of four sides measuring 2 inches each, can be described variously as an 8-inch, a 4-inch or a 2-inch knot to knot. The usual and most understandable way is to call it a 4-inch. This means that a thin 4-inch wide flat gauge could be passed through the mesh when the net was wet. This is the checking method used by the authorities, and to be on the safe side it may be as well to order the mesh on the easy side, although net makers usually allow for this.

Much against my master's advice, I tried trawling, but due to the rough terrain of my fishing parish, it turned out, as Twm warned, a heart- and back-breaking business. True, I found small patches of clear, fish-holding ground, but the effort of shooting and hauling so often was not worth the effort, and it was abandoned for more productive pursuits.

Since then I have done quite a bit of trawling in other areas, both offshore and inshore as guest crew, with varied results, so do not let my local failure be too discouraging. It is only a matter of finding a suitable fish-holding bottom and a deal of know-how.

For the tyro who is fishing for the cooking pot, I think the most easily worked gear is a small beam trawl. It consists of a wooden or pipe beam with sledge-like irons at either end. The beam keeps the bag-like net open lengthwise, and the irons keep the mouth open and help the gear to slide over the ground. The footrope is heavily weighted to enable it to hug the bottom and stir up the flatfish.

Fixing the Trawl

The other type of trawl is known as the "otter". It has the advantage of having no cumbersome beam and, correctly rigged, gives a much wider mouth opening than the beam type, and is considerably more productive. It relies on a pair of "otters" that work on the principle of children's kites, but instead of the two-point bridle in a kite, the otter is held at four points, which are adjustable to control vertical spreading angles.

My first attempts at adjustment were catastrophic, and remained so until I hit on the idea of watching the net's behaviour by towing a dinghy directly over it in shallow, clear water. By this method it was possible to adjust the otters to give maximum spread, and balance this against engine power.

If the trawl bug bites, my advice would be to take heed of local knowledge and when ordering gear let the makers know the size of boat, and the power and type of engine. Suppliers' addresses can be obtained in that useful and informative weekly paper, "Fishing News". This paper has an excellent advisory technical team who have come up the hard way. They are presided over by Commander John Burgess, one-time inshoreman, and writer of the book, "Escape to Sea".

Here are a few basic knots with the accent on those that are easily released. Without the slightest doubt, the most useful of them all is the bowline. The advantage is that whatever strain is put on it, it can be cast off with a flick of the thumb. Another point in its favour is that it only reduces the rope's breaking strain by 10 per cent, whereas other knots, notably the so-called fisherman's bend or anchor hitch, are reputed to reduce the breaking strain by 70 per cent. Rather a thought when one's boat or net is hanging to the anchor for dear life. Peace of mind can be obtained if the rope first takes two round turns around the ring and finishes with a bowline with the spare end tucked through the rope's lay.

Knots and Nets

The reef knot as a temporary fastening should be avoided where there is strain as, when wet, it is almost impossible to

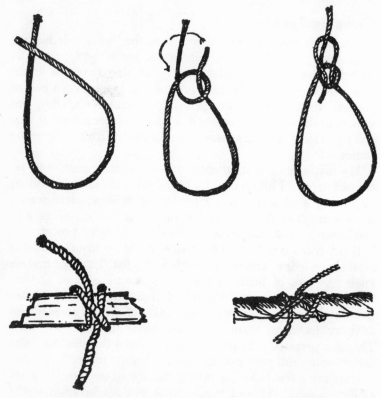

FIG. 29. Basic knots. Bowline, Clove hitch and Rolling hitch.

release. A most useful knot is the sheet bend, or netting knot. It is nearly as easy to cast off as a bowline. For permanent hitching, such as slinging a sheet of net between ropes, two half-hitches known as the clove (see Fig. 29) are used, but three are better. A similar sort of knot, known as the rolling or un-slipable hitch (see Fig. 29), is used to fixhook-carrying snoods

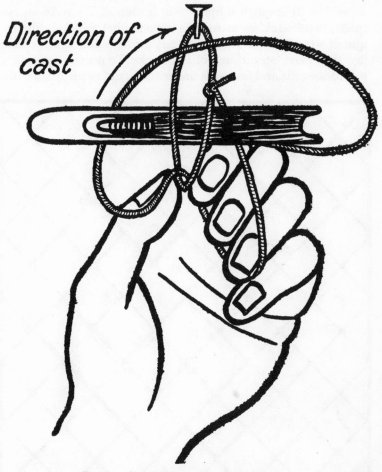

Direction of cast

FIG. 30. Showing formation of netting knot.
(Adapted from W. S. Forsyth's "Inshore Fishing".)

to long lines. There are many other types of knot but it is possible to get by with the few described. Proficiency will not be obtained until they can be tied with hands behind the back— even more difficult than in the dark.

Splicing is a simple operation. In joining two ropes together, first unlay the ends for about 8 inches, marry them together, and tie opposing strands with, as it were, the first part of a reef knot, then tuck spare ends of strands through and against the ropes' lay. It is much simpler than it sounds. To make an eye splice, bend back on to rope to a point that will give the required size of eye and push strands through and against each lay, then carry on tucking for four tucks. To neaten any splice, roll backwards and forwards under foot, cutting off spare ends.

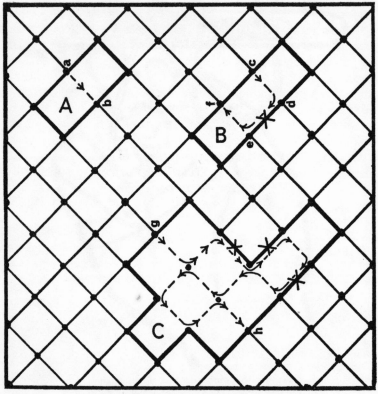

FIG. 31. Mending tears.
(Adapted from W. S. Forsyth's "Inshore Fishing".)

My advice is not to bother about net making—leave it to the machine and the construction to the makers. It is, however, necessary to have some knowledge of the simpler repairs. The only tool required is a needle that will pass through the mesh and carry the twine (see Fig. 30). Needles range upwards in size from the tiny ones for shrimp mesh, and are best bought over the counter. The knot used is a sheet bend, and the diagram (see Fig. 31) will give some idea of how to deal with three types of tears. Should tears be larger than those shown, lay the net out flat and do some hard thinking, along the lines of tear C. Tear A is easily dealt with by starting and finishing with a double sheet bend. It is necessary to double knot at start and finish points, otherwise the knot will slip. In B, where two strands are broken, cut out bar marked X and start at (c) on to (d), then (e) and finish at (f). Tear C calls for three bars to be cut out (marked by X). Start at (g), follow the arrows and finish at (h). The reason for cutting odd bars out is that it makes a neater repair by using one length of twine. Liken net mending to a game of draughts played with a bit of string, and you won't go far wrong. Your early attempts may have a crazy paving look, but they will close the hole which, after all, is all that matters.

Having discussed some of the technicalities of catching and dressing, it is time for me to lash down and stow, handing over to "herself", who will close with, possibly, the most important chapter.

Chapter 18

Winning Full Profit from Your Catch

BEING the working partner to an inshoreman can be a hard life but infinitely interesting and rewarding. Adaptability is the operative word, as life during the busy fishing season can be a hectic affair. House, crew work and sleep all have to be fitted into fishing times and tides. I soon realised that, apart from the time I was seaborne, many other jobs come my way, including re-fitting, picking nets and tearing round in a Land Rover selling the catch. I was indeed glad to welcome our partnership with Huw as I now have more time to give to the preparation and cooking of the sea food which, being free, is our main diet. This ranges from a soup made with gatherings from the seashore and rock pools, to a smoked salmon sandwich.

Although all prime fish goes for sale, there is no shortage of what we called "rubbish". By this I mean lobsters and crabs that have been fighting in the pot with subsequent loss of limbs, and the less saleable sorts of fish, which require cooking with imagination. I experimented with them all and learnt many useful tips and at times earned approbation from "himself" who is quite a connoisseur in these matters.

In selecting a lobster, whether alive or cooked, grip firmly across the carapace or shoulders, which should be absolutely firm and unyielding. If there is any inward movement of the fingers it points to a recent shell change and consequent loss of meat, and the lobster should be discarded. If there are a few barnacles on the shell so much the better. A cock lobster has large claws and a narrow body while the hen has a wider body and smaller claws, but from a culinary viewpoint there is no difference. To cook a lobster, plunge it into boiling, very salty water—sea water, plus salt, if possible. Allow to come back to the boil and then simmer for twenty minutes for the first pound, and ten minutes for every subsequent pound. Cool naturally.

Never put a lobster in a fridge otherwise it will dehydrate and lose its delicate taste.

For later eye-appeal, rub the shell with a butter paper. Remove the claws and crack with a flat stone to avoid chipping. With a sharp knife open down the back, remove the dark, intestinal thread, the stomach, which is like a small paper bag behind the nose, and the gills. Arrange the opened halves on a bed of lettuce surrounded with the crushed claws, and serve with a simple salad, thin brown bread and butter and home-made mayonnaise and, if possible, provide that useful tool, a lobster pick. In this form it is worthy of a good white wine preferably Chablis of French extraction.

Making One Small Lobster Go Far

Although, in my opinion, this is the best way to eat a lobster, there are some simple economical ways of making a small lobster serve several people. Here is one method. Cook as above, remove all the flesh from the body and claws and put aside. Discard the stomach and gills and then simmer the empty shell in milk and water for about half an hour. Make a well seasoned white sauce using the lobster stock, a few drops of anchovy essence and a squeeze of lemon. Add the lobster, cut into small pieces, reheat and fill the washed shells, sprinkle with brown breadcrumbs, a little grated cheese and a dab of butter and put under the grill or in a hot oven to brown. This can be stretched even further by putting the mixture in a bed of mashed potatoes or rice in an ovenproof dish or scallop shells and browning in the same way.

Lobster flesh can also be treated like scampi. Cut into pieces, egg and breadcrumb and fry, preferably in butter. Serve with a mayonnaise sauce to which has been added chopped chives or capers. Lobster is also a most useful addition to rice dishes such as Spanish Paella.

We had a plentiful supply of crabs but they were not always welcome as they were inclined to take possession of a pot and keep lobsters out. Not always welcome, either, in the kitchen

186

as the preparation and dressing is a patient, rather tedious, chore but the result is infinitely worthwhile. They should be selected for their weight in proportion to their size, hardness of shell and size of claw. The crab differs from the lobster in that it must be left in cold salted water for about half an hour before heat is applied. Cooking time is the same as for lobsters. When cold twist off claws and legs and with the crab on its back, prise open the apron with a pointed knife, and remove body portion. Discard the stomach bag near the mouth, and the grey gills known as "dead man's fingers". Remove all the flesh from the honeycomb-like sections with a skewer or lobster pick, and put in a basin with the meat from the claws. Add about a tablespoonful of fine white breadcrumbs, pepper, salt, chopped parsley, made mustard and a little vinegar, taking care not to make it too wet. In another basin mash the dark meat from inside the shell, add a few white breadcrumbs and season. Wash and dry the empty shell and rub with a buttered paper for an attractive finish. Put the white meat down each side of the shell, and the dark meat, coated with mayonnaise, down the centre. Decorate with chopped parsley, paprika pepper and the meat pushed out of the legs. Care should be taken to avoid getting any small shell splinter or transparent sinews mixed with the meat.

Crab Meat Made Tasty

A pleasant change from cold dressed crab is to use the meat from a couple of medium-sized crabs as follows. Roughly chop the crab meat, a few mushrooms, a peeled tomato and a small onion and fry together gently in 1 oz. of melted butter for ten minutes. Season with salt and black pepper and add a little top-of-the-milk. Pile into the washed and glazed shells, sprinkle with brown breadcrumbs, add a knob of butter, brown under the grill and serve decorated with chopped parsley.

Mussels have been plentiful and our great stand-by, both as a meal and as an attractive addition to various fish and meat dishes. It is important to cleanse mussels carefully by soaking in cold salty water for at least an hour, discarding any with opened shells, then washing in several changes of water to get rid of any grit.

Undoubtedly Moules à la Marinière is the most superb way

of cooking a dish of mussels. Tip the clean mussels into a large pan (without water) and boil fiercely for ten minutes. Pour off liquor and place aside for a few minutes to allow any specks of sand or shell to settle. Pour liquor into another saucepan and add half a glass of white wine—or, if preferred, a smaller quantity of vinegar—together with a clove of garlic and a chopped onion. Allow to reduce for a few minutes, then thicken slightly with a mixture of butter and flour, and add chopped parsley. Place mussels, still in shell, in a deep soup-plate or bowl and pour the liquor over them. Eat with lots of crusty bread, a spoon, and finger and thumb. Once having acquired the taste, there are few fish dishes that are not improved by the addition of a handful of mussels. Try them, also, in a steak pudding.

Scallops were never plentiful on our part of the coast, but were occasionally picked up after a northerly blow. To open, put them in a moderate oven for a few minutes, then with a knife gently prise open. Rinse them, still in their shells, under running cold water to remove any mud or sand, then take out the scallop, taking care not to detach the orange-coloured roe. Remove any black parts and "beards" and scrub the empty shells. There are various ways of cooking them.

To bake, line the deep shell with seasoned white breadcrumbs, place a scallop on top, cover with more breadcrumbs, a squeeze of lemon juice and a tablespoonful of melted butter. Bake in a moderate oven for about twenty minutes and serve in the shells garnished with parsley and paprika.

Scallops are Delicious

Another method is to simmer the de-shelled scallops in milk for five or ten minutes according to size. Make a well-seasoned cheese sauce using the flavoured milk. Put a layer of sauce in each deep shell, place a scallop on top, and cover with more of the sauce, leaving the orange row uncovered for eye-appeal. Sprinkle with a mixture of breadcrumbs and finely grated cheese and a knob of butter. Pipe mashed potatoes round each shell and brown under the grill or in a hot oven.

A good rice dish can be made from odds and ends collected from the seashore and rock pools, including mussels, cockles, shrimps and prawns, and any left-over morsels of lobster and crab. First boil a panful of Patna rice, preferably in stock from mussels, etc. Drain well, and put aside to keep hot. In a large frying pan toss a lump of butter, two onions, two tomatoes, a few mushrooms if available, and a crushed clove of garlic. Fry for ten minutes, adding salt and black pepper to taste. Add the rice and heat thoroughly. Then fold in the cooked and prepared beach gatherings, keeping back a few unshelled shrimps and prawns for decoration. Serve very hot.

Our off-season stand-by was various dishes, including dog and pollack that we had dry-salted in times of plenty. From a culinary viewpoint their use was fairly limited and, of course, quite uncookable until they had been de-salted by soaking in water overnight. This done, they can be mixed with an equal quantity of mashed potato, with some chopped parsley added, together with a dash of mixed herbs and garlic if you like it. We do. Then make into rissoles, coat with egg and breadcrumb and fry. Another way of using de-salted fish is to cut it into small slabs, place in a baking tin, cover with a tin of tomatoes, an egg-cup full of vinegar, black pepper, garlic, or onion, to taste. Allow to bubble away gently for an hour.

Home Smoked Supply

Occasionally, we smoked a small supply of fish including herring, mackerel, whiting and sea trout. These were for our own consumption, and generally speaking the end product was not up to professional standard in looks, but it certainly tasted good. As the fish were only lightly salted before smoking, we were able to keep them, in a cool place, for only a week or so. Cooking was limited to placing them in hot water for a few minutes, drying and brushing over with melted butter, and as the smoking had done most of the cooking, grilling either side for a very short time.

During the summer, usually in the holiday season, there occurs a glut of mackerel. Try this easy way of gutting and filleting in two cuts. Lay the fish flat and cut gently behind the head until the backbone is felt. Then turn the knife and cut tailwards, pressing flat on the backbone. Reverse fish and re-peat, and the result is two oval fillets that are manageable in the pan and on the plate.

One's stomach rapidly rebels against anything in the shape

of the grilled or fried variety, but luckily there are other more digestive ways of dealing with them. Head, tail and clean fish, fill with a thyme and parsley stuffing, sprinkle with salt, black pepper, dot with butter and bake, covered with a buttered paper.

Our favourite, and quite the simplest way of cooking mackerel, is to simmer gently in a little salted water to which has been added half a dozen sprigs of mint and a little vinegar. Any surplus fish can be filleted, cleaned, rolled and soused as one would herrings.

In the early days of our endeavours we were literally knee-deep in herring during the season, but nowadays the shoals give our waters a miss; so much so that it is useless to wet a net. We can still enjoy herrings ex-shop, if they are prepared to the following instructions, given us by a Swedish fisherman.

Have ready in a deep dish the following mixture: 1 cup vinegar, 1 cup water, ½ cup sugar, 2 sliced onions, salt and a few crushed peppercorns. De-bone, scale and make herrings into meat fillets. Dip in seasoned flour and fry lightly in hot oil. When cooked and drained, put at once, while hot, into the pickle and leave for twelve hours. Remove, and store in a cool place where they will keep up to a week.

One Dish of Great Merit

As a tailpiece to my "do it yourself" cookery, I will end with a dish of great merit. It's only connection with the sea is that it was learned from the skipper-cum-cook of a French crabber who fishes for lobsters in our part of the Irish Sea.

Toss a lump of butter into a skillet and frizzle some small pieces of bacon. Cover with grated cheese and drench with top-of-the-milk. When bubbling, break in the required number of eggs, baste, cover with a lid and allow to poach. Serve on a raft of fried bread. Truly delicious.

I am indeed fortunate with my raw materials. Shop-bought products, possibly caught weeks before, and kept at varying temperatures on ice, are a mere shadow of the inshoreman's fresh and tasteful wares.

If I had my time over again I would choose no other way of life. So full of contrasts, ranging from blissfully busy days at sea with weather and catch going our way, to other times when one is miserably cold, wet and occasionally very frightened. Another compensation is that the work is seasonal, leaving the winter for other ploys, including passaging towards the Spanish sun where we manage to live economically and pay our way with a pen.

Marketing the Catch

In order to give fishermen practical points on marketing their catch to best advantage, the advice and help of Billingsgate experts was sought.

Through the good offices of the Secretary of the London Fish Merchants' Association, Mr. T. J. Phillips, the co-operation of Mr. Peter Witchell, Director of B. H. Witt Ltd., was secured. In terms of quantity handled, his Company is one of the top three firms in Billingsgate dealing in these crustaceans. Other merchants of course also handle them and, to avoid discrimination, a list of all the main operators is given at the end of this article together with their telephone numbers—this last for a reason that is brought out in the detailed advice given.

Billingsgate, of course, is the main inland market in the U.K. because of its geographical position, the innumerable outlets provided by a dense population, and its ability to meet all demands in quantity and quality with speed and reliability; but it may suit some producers to endeavour to secure outlets in some of the larger provincial centres.

The number of suppliers sending consignments forward to Billingsgate runs into the hundreds and possibly the thousands—regular consignments from points all round the coasts of Britain and Ireland. From the detailed points made by Mr. Witchell and Mr. Phillips, suppliers stand to benefit substantially in monetary returns by giving greater heed to the following recommendations, based on long experience:

Containers

Consignments reach Billingsgate in all sorts of containers, but the greater proportion from regular suppliers comes forward in lightweight tea chests into which about 1 cwt. of lobsters and crabs can be packed. This container is popular because of its light tare (about 12 to 14 lb.) in relation to the weight contained and the freight rate charged.

For convenience in handling by porters at Billingsgate, boxes of 4–5 stone in weight do find favour in the market, but from the producer's angle, the tea chest is preferred. It is light but still strong enough to withstand the inevitable bumping of transport. In general, tea chests are not returned to consignors, who make their own arrangements for obtaining them from the nearest local sources. This is because the cost of return is prohibitive.

Grading

The action by which suppliers can do most to improve their own cash returns is by grading their lobsters and crabs as evenly as possible to sizes and nature.

The ideal grading for lobsters is this:

(1) ¾ lb. to 1 lb.
(2) 1 lb. to 2¼ lb.
(3) 2½ lb. to 3½ lb.
(4) over 3½ lb.—so called "giants".

"Cripples"—that is, lobsters with one claw missing—should be included in the category 2½ lb. to 3½ lb. regardless of their size as their value is roughly the same.

Well graded even lines help the merchants secure good prices because the buyer is assured of even quality without re-handling and selection. The range of prices secured by these categories runs thus: top price is secured for the 1 lb.–2¼ lb. lobsters. The next best price is for ¾ lb. to 1 lb.; then come the 2½ lb.–3½ lb. fish, while the giants—over 3½ lb.—go to the bottom of the table. Prices naturally vary from day to day according to supply and demand.

In the summer, when supplies are at their peak, up to 25 per cent of arrivals may be sold by the box, the price being governed by the size and weight of the contents—a good reason for proper grading.

It is the merchant's business to secure the highest price he can for the benefit of his suppliers. He is governed by two factors—the demand from buyers and the volume of supply. Buyers, when inspecting a box that has not been graded, will naturally base their valuation on the poorest specimens and try to get the lot at a low price. The merchant, working for the producers, will of course point out the better fish and stress the quality of the average of the box.

It pays therefore, to have an even range of sizes and quality wherever possible. That benefits the merchant, saves time, impresses the buyer and gives the producer a generally better average return.

In the winter, when supplies are smaller, grading is of course less easy and the merchant must then do the best he can for his client by himself grading and endeavouring to organise even lines. This point about grading was emphasised time and again by Mr. Witchell on behalf of the merchants of Billingsgate as being the one big thing a producer can do to help himself get the best return for his produce.

Packing

The method of packing lobsters in their container is also of great importance. Probably the best medium in which to pack them is good dry wood wool. This is absolutely ideal.

The next best medium is dry sawdust. Its use, however, is attended by one very great danger unless outstanding care is taken. While it is reasonably absorbent, the slightest excess of water drip turns the sawdust into a solid lump which stifles the lobster right away. And a dead lobster is of much less value on the market.

Seaweed is not recommended as a packing medium because it is too heavy for a start, and damp. Grass is the very worst packing medium in the world because it generates heat.

Ice is a wonderful help in good packing but it must be used properly. The best thing is to get a polythene bag, put the ice in and tie the neck with a simple knot. Thus handled, the ice lasts longer and if it does melt, the water is kept away from the other packing and the lobster arrives dry.

Flake ice is preferred to crushed ice because it moulds itself in size and shape to the requirements of the pack—but it must always be put in a polythene bag, well tied.

In the absence of ice, packers should use the best packing material they can get. Packing the lobster dry is an important point.

When supplies are short, some producers keep a few days' catch in a box submerged in the water until they get enough to make up a consignment. Then they will be taken out and while still wet packed into tea chests or containers and away they go. That is not good practice. The lobster should be dried to a reasonable extent before being packed.

These recommended methods are all tried and proved; they are based on experience. It may be that packing with some of the new plastic materials now coming on the market may prove beneficial and be worth investigating but, so far as is now known, no experiments in this direction have been made and consignors contemplating the use of such new materials would be well advised to consult their merchant beforehand so that experiments can be carefully watched.

The cardinal point to remember always is that carelessness in grading and packing means less money for the consignment.

Timing the Market Needs

Suppliers could benefit themselves very considerably by endeavouring to have their consignments reach the market on the best day of the week and, above all, by advising their merchants beforehand as to the nature of the consignment they are sending forward.

The best prices tend to be secured early in the week on Mondays, Tuesdays and Wednesdays, with the emphasis on Tuesdays, as the best day. By Wednesday, supplies are increasing and Thursday is generally a flood day when supplies are heaviest and consequently the price tends to drop. Friday sometimes shows a good demand but on a broad average early in the week is the best time for the producers to get good prices.

Buyers of course keep in close touch with the market and ask the merchant what supplies are coming forward. It is therefore of great advantage to the merchants and the market to have early advice.

The best way of ensuring this is by using the telephone. Wherever possible producers are recommended to make arrangements with their merchants by telephoning the night before at cheap rate times and saying what supplies are going forward.

Some producers are meticulous in giving this early advice but not enough use the telephone. Postal advice does not arrive early enough for a market that opens at 6 a.m. Some suppliers have been known to despatch a consignment by air and then carefully post off advice which invariably arrives at least twenty-four hours after the consignment.

To facilitate receipt of telephone advice, some merchants have installed recording machines which will automatically take down and play back the next morning messages received at night rate. With the steady expansion of dialling systems this method is likely to be considerably expanded. That will facilitate the effort of the producer to give the merchant early advice and reduce cost. In any case, most merchants are only too pleased to arrange to receive advice by telephone at home during the evening when the cheap rate applies.

Arrival of consignments at railhead in London presents no trouble. Collection and delivery arrangements from railhead to Billingsgate are well organised and every consignment is picked up promptly on arrival and delivered to the market.

Summing up, Monday is generally notable for almost complete lack of supply. Tuesday is about the best day for good demand; Wednesday and more particularly Thursday, the market tends to be heavily supplied.

The lesson from the foregoing is therefore that better prices are likely to be secured by deliveries made early in the week. Spreading deliveries will take the pressure off the market later in the week and will encourage better prices generally.

Crabs

Grading should be carried out with crabs as well. The hens should be separated from the cocks and the latter graded between large and small. Large crabs range from 4 to 7 lb. and small up to about $3\frac{1}{2}$ lb. Cock crabs invariably bring more money than hen crabs.

Spider crabs have little value and are not worth sending as a separate line. If, however, they can be included as make-weights—for instance to fill up the last 10 or 12 lb. in a cwt. consignment, they are then worth sending.

Spider crabs in the U.K. are not as big as the famous Alaskan king crabs which measure up to 3 or 4 feet across. It is the meat from those long spider legs that is packed in tins and marketed in Britain.

Crawfish

The supply of crawfish reaching the market is very small and the demand is limited. Actually the out-turn of meat from a crawfish is really slightly better than from a lobster, but it is not yet popular on the British market, although on the Continental market it is quite a different story.

List of Billingsgate Merchants dealing in Lobsters, Crabs and Crawfish

Associated Fisheries and Foods (Bennett) Ltd.	35 Monument Street, London, E.C.3.	01-626 8433
Bacon, G. A. (Billingsgate) Ltd.	2 Billingsgate Market, London, E.C.3.	01-626 0960
Baxter & Son, Ltd.	15/16 Billingsgate Market, London, E.C.3.	01-623 9144
Bloomfield, R. Ltd.	34 Fish Street Hill, London, E.C.3.	01-626 7749
Brice Bros. Ltd.	52/54 Billingsgate Market, London, E.C.3.	01-626 4925

Bush, T. (Billingsgate) Ltd.	183/184 Billingsgate Market, London, E.C.3.	01-623 5651
Fisher Bros. & Co. (Shellfish) Ltd.	12 Billingsgate Market, London, E.C.3.	01-626 6694
Joscelyne, E. & Sons Ltd.	83/84 Billingsgate Market, London, E.C.3.	01-626 1016
Leleu & Morris, Ltd.	118 Billingsgate Market, London, E.C.3.	01-626 3761
Maynard, A. E. Ltd.	34 Monument Street, London, E.C.3.	01-626 4703
Nye, C. H. Ltd.	253/4 Billingsgate Market, London, E.C.3.	01-626 8929
Scutt, Sam Ltd.	51 Monument Street, London, E.C.3.	01-626 1908
Street, Alfred & Co. Ltd.	18/19 Billingsgate Market, London, E.C.3.	01-626 2150
Witt, B. H. Ltd.	245 Billingsgate Market, London, E.C.3.	01-626 1773
Wombwell, C.	31/33 Billingsgate Buildings, London, E.C.3.	01-626 7320
Wright, Thomas M. (Billingsgate) Ltd.	10 Billingsgate Market, London, E.C.3.	01-626 6750

Berried Lobsters

As from July 1, 1966, the ban on the landing and selling of berried lobsters carrying spawn was lifted. That ban was originally imposed under the Sea Fishing Industry (Crabs and Lobsters) Order, 1951, in the belief that it would conserve the stocks of lobsters. Scientific evidence since has indicated that it has not been effective for that purpose and consequently the ban has now been removed.

As a result of this removal, the supply of hen lobsters to the market since July 1966 has improved and the expectation is that further increase will be maintained.

The minimum size of lobsters that can be marketed remains unaltered in the new Order at 9 inches but the method of measurement has been changed to read "from the tip of the beak to the end of the shell of the centre flap of the tail". This is because the former method was insufficiently precise. The minimum size of crabs permitted to be landed remains at $4\frac{1}{2}$ inches across the broadest part of the back.